COMPREHENSIVE RESEARCH
AND STUDY GUIDE

John
Keats

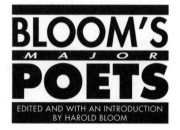

BLOOM'S
MAJOR
POETS

EDITED AND WITH AN INTRODUCTION
BY HAROLD BLOOM

BLOOM'S MAJOR SHORT STORY WRITERS

Anton Chekhov

Joseph Conrad

Stephen Crane

William Faulkner

F. Scott Fitzgerald

Nathaniel Hawthorne

Ernest Hemingway

O. Henry

Shirley Jackson

Henry James

James Joyce

D. H. Lawrence

Jack London

Herman Melville

Flannery O'Connor

Edgar Allan Poe

Katherine Anne Porter

J. D. Salinger

John Steinbeck

Mark Twain

John Updike

Eudora Welty

BLOOM'S MAJOR WORLD POETS

Maya Angelou

Robert Browning

Geoffrey Chaucer

Samuel T. Coleridge

Dante

Emily Dickinson

John Donne

T. S. Eliot

Robert Frost

Homer

Langston Hughes

John Keats

John Milton

Sylvia Plath

Edgar Allan Poe

Poets of World War I

Shakespeare's Poems
 & Sonnets

Percy Shelley

Alfred, Lord Tennyson

Walt Whitman

William Wordsworth

William Butler Yeats

John
Keats

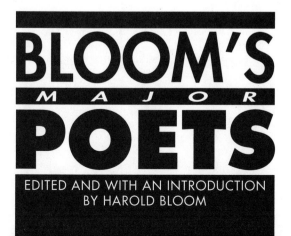

BLOOM'S *MAJOR*
POETS

© 2001 by Chelsea House Publishers, a subsidiary of
Haights Cross Communications.

Introduction © 2001 by Harold Bloom.

Printed and bound in the United States of America.

First Printing
1 3 5 7 9 8 6 4 2

Library of Congress Cataloging-in-Publication Data

John Keats / editor, Harold Bloom.
        p.   cm.—(Bloom's major poets)
    ISBN 0-7910-5934-0 (alk. paper)
        1. Keats, John, 1795–1821—Criticism and interpretation—
Handbooks, manuals, etc. 2. Keats, John, 1795–1821—Examinations—
Study guides.
        I. Bloom, Harold. II. Series.

PR4837.J57   2000
821'.7—dc21   00-064453
                                               CIP

Chelsea House Publishers
1974 Sproul Road, Suite 400
Broomall, PA 19008-0914

The Chelsea House World Wide Web address is
http://www.chelseahouse.com

Contributing Editor: Janyce Marson

Produced by: Robert Gerson Publisher's Services, Santa Barbara, CA

Contents

User's Guide

This volume is designed to present biographical, critical, and bibliographical information on the author's best-known or most important poems. Following Harold Bloom's editor's note and introduction is a detailed biography of the author, discussing major life events and important literary accomplishments. A thematic and structural analysis of each poem follows, tracing significant themes, patterns, and motifs in the work.

A selection of critical extracts, derived from previously published material from leading critics, analyzes aspects of each poem. The extracts consist of statements from the author, if available, early reviews of the work, and later evaluations up to the present. A bibliography of the author's writings (including a complete list of all books written, cowritten, edited, and translated), a list of additional books and articles on the author and the work, and an index of themes and ideas in the author's writings conclude the volume.

Harold Bloom is Sterling Professor of the Humanities at Yale University and Henry W. and Albert A. Berg Professor of English at the New York University Graduate School. He is the author of over 20 books, including *Shelley's Mythmaking* (1959), *The Visionary Company* (1961), *Blake's Apocalypse* (1963), *Yeats* (1970), *A Map of Misreading* (1975), *Kabbalah and Criticism* (1975), *Agon: Toward a Theory of Revisionism* (1982), *The American Religion* (1992), *The Western Canon* (1994), and *Omens of Millennium: The Gnosis of Angels, Dreams, and Resurrection* (1996). *The Anxiety of Influence* (1973) sets forth Professor Bloom's provocative theory of the literary relationships between the great writers and their predecessors. His most recent books include *Shakespeare: The Invention of the Human*, a 1998 National Book Award finalist, and *How to Read and Why*, which was published in 2000.

Professor Bloom earned his Ph.D. from Yale University in 1955 and has served on the Yale faculty since then. He is a 1985 MacArthur Foundation Award recipient, served as the Charles Eliot Norton Professor of Poetry at Harvard University in 1987–88, and has received honorary degrees from the universities of Rome and Bologna. In 1999, Professor Bloom received the prestigious American Academy of Arts and Letters Gold Medal for Criticism.

Currently, Harold Bloom is the editor of numerous Chelsea House volumes of literary criticism, including the series BLOOM'S NOTES, BLOOM'S MAJOR DRAMATISTS, BLOOM'S MAJOR NOVELISTS, MAJOR LITERARY CHARACTERS, MODERN CRITICAL VIEWS, MODERN CRITICAL INTERPRETATIONS, and WOMEN WRITERS OF ENGLISH AND THEIR WORKS.

Editor's Note

My Introduction is an appreciation of Keats's artistry in the Great Odes, and concludes with the Shakespearean element in his final poems.

The critical views are all of great usefulness and distinction, and I will indicate only a few nuances here.

Aileen Ward illuminates the relation of "Ode on a Grecian Urn" to the visual arts, while Jacqueline Banerjee points to Shakespeare in "The Eve of St. Agnes."

The "Ode to a Nightingale" is related by Cynthia Chase to the traditional poetic gesture of flower-naming, after which Paul D. Sheats considers the genre of the poem.

"To Autumn," perhaps Keats's masterpiece, is seen by all the essayists as a vision of mortality, while Grant T. Webster establishes a Dantesque presence in "La Belle Dame Sans Merci."

Introduction

HAROLD BLOOM

John Keats is unique among all major poets after Shakespeare in that his consciousness is so profoundly normative; that is, it is so natural, sane, sympathetic, balanced, and equable as to give us an example of what human life can be at its most wise and compassionate. A normative person is very rare, whether in life or in literature, and this rareness enhances Keats's value for us, as a poet and as a human being.

Keats died at twenty-five and left us a truncated canon. His two major long poems—*Hyperion* and *The Fall of Hyperion*—are fragments, but they manifest a greatness that transcends his art in the Great Odes, the sonnets and major lyrics, and in *Lamia* and *The Eve of St. Agnes*.

Here I desire only to note a few of the particular excellences of the Great Odes, and of the astonishing ballad, "La Belle Dame Sans Merci." The most famous of the Odes is "On a Grecian Urn," which has haunted poetic tradition down to its reappearance in Wallace Stevens's "The Poems of Our Climate," where Keats's powerful estrangement: "Thou, silent form, doth tease us out of thought / as doth eternity: Cold pastoral" is echoed as: "cold, a cold porcelain." It is strikingly bitter that Keats becomes more and more distant from what he contemplates upon the urn as the poem proceeds. This is akin to the transition from the last line of stanza VII to the opening of stanza VIII in the "Ode to a Nightingale." "Faery lands forlorn" leads to the tolling of the word, "forlorn," like a bell, as Keats is tolled back from the state of being one with the nightingale's song to the isolation of "my sole self."

I have a personal preference for the "Ode to Psyche" and the "Ode on Melancholy," but would have to grant that the superb "To Autumn" is probably the most eminent of the Great Odes of Keats. But, in these poems, we choose among sublimities:

> Sometimes whoever seeks abroad may find
> Thee sitting careless on a granary floor,
> Thy hair soft-lifted by the winnowing wind;

Keats's harvest-girl, profoundly erotic, lingers half-way between Milton's Eve and Tennyson's Mariana. The influence of Keats has been enormous; he fostered not only Tennyson and the pre-Raphaelites, but rather more subtly helped to form Emily Dickinson's oxymoronic rhetoric. Keats has remained a presence in subsequent American poetry from Trumboll Stickney, Wallace Stevens, and Hart Crane on to the remarkable Henri Cole, one of the most accomplished of our contemporary poets. In England, Keats fathered Wilfred Owen, the great poet of World War I, while in Ireland his effect lingered always upon William Butler Yeats.

In his closing days, Keats began a crucial transition from his agon with Milton and with Wordsworth to a larger, loving contest with Shakespeare. The sonnet "On the Sea" suggests *King Lear*'s: "When last the winds of Heaven were unbound," while Keats's final fragment could be inserted in many Shakespearean contexts and be altogether at home, in its power of apprehension and its eloquence:

> This living hand, now warm and capable
> Of earnest grasping, would, if it were cold
> And in the icy silence of the tomb,
> So haunt thy days and chill thy dreaming nights
> That thou wouldst wish thine own heart dry of blood
> So in my veins red life might stream again,
> And thou be conscience-calm'd—see here it is—
> I hold it towards you. ☸

Biography of
John Keats

Throughout his life, John Keats lived with a foreboding sense of his own early death. This fear no doubt contributed to the rapid pace at which he produced his best work.

The roots of Keats's fears about death are to be found in his early childhood. His father, Thomas Keats, originally the head stableman at a London livery stable, had risen from a humble background to become a prosperous businessman. When he was thrown from a horse on the evening of April 15, 1804, he sustained a fatal skull fracture and died the following morning. Keats was only eight years old at the time.

His mother, Frances Keats, now an attractive young widow left with the responsibility for four young children and a thriving business, hastily remarried two months later on June 27, 1804. But the marriage did not last, and when she left her new husband, William Rawlings, the laws of the day forced her to relinquish all claim to her property and legal control of her children. Keats's maternal grandmother, Alice Jennings, took custody of the four children, Tom, George, John, and Fanny, while Frances disappeared for several years to live with a man named Abraham. During this time, she began to drink heavily, and when she returned a few years later to her family in Edmonton, she was ill and bedridden, though she was still only in her early thirties. Keats, an adolescent by now, gazed painfully upon her faded beauty and vitality. In March of 1810, he received news of his mother's death from tuberculosis, a disease that at the time was poorly understood, though it ran rampant in London.

Her death had a profound influence on Keats, transforming him from an irresponsible boy who loved to joke with his friends and get involved in brawls to a quiet young man who became passionately absorbed in reading. When his younger brother Tom also contracted tuberculosis in 1818, Keats suspected that this would be the last of the anguished farewells he would have to endure before his own untimely death. He was very close to Tom, and he took his brother to Margate, a popular resort on the coast of Kent, hoping that the sea air would improve Tom's health. Keats cared for his brother devotedly during his final months, but eventually Tom succumbed to the disease. Keats was still in good health, but his brother's death left him with a profound consciousness that he too might not have much longer to live.

Other aspects of Keats's life were not as dark. His early education was at John Clarke's academy in Enfield. Clarke, a trained lawyer, found teaching far more satisfying than the law. He was a man of liberal convictions who remained steadfast even when the public turned against him during the political turbulence of the 1790s. Clarke was friends with radical reformers such as John Cartwright, a Parliamentary reformer, and Joseph Priestley, a scientist and Unitarian minister.

At Enfield, Keats received an enlightened education. The village itself was the perfect environment for a schoolboy with its rolling fields, shady woods, and river in which to swim. Keats was a high-spirited young boy, fond of skylarking and fistfights. While at Enfield, Keats probably developed his close and loving knowledge of fruits and flowers. And most important, at Enfield in the summer of 1803 he made the acquaintance of Cowden Clarke, the headmaster's son. Cowden Clarke became his teacher, and later, in the course of their friendship, he introduced Keats to Spenser, to tales of romantic adventure and chivalrous deeds, and to the music of Mozart and Handel. Years later, Cowden Clarke recalled Keats reading a handbook on classical mythology. This interest led him to do a voluntary prose translation of the *Aeneid* in his last year at Enfield. Clarke also influenced Keats's interest in politics, lending the young poet copies of *The Examiner* (the leading liberal magazine of the day) and helping him to form his opinion about the injustices in the world around him.

However, Keats's education soon took an abrupt turn when Richard Abbey, the Keats children's guardian, assumed responsibility at the direction of their grandmother, the aging Alice Jennings. Abbey, a prosperous tea broker, landowner, and churchwarden, had known Mrs. Jennings quite well. He was also unimaginative and practical-minded, and when Keats was fifteen years of age, Abbey decided to bind the young poet as an apprentice to Thomas Hammond, a surgeon and apothecary at Edmonton.

At that time, the apothecaries were of the lowest rank in the medical hierarchy. In fact, not until 1745 did the surgeons break away from the medieval guild of Barbers and Surgeons and begin to establish criteria of their own. In 1815, Keats left Thomas Hammond to enter the United Hospitals of Guy's and St. Thomas's. He was a full-fledged medical student now, and here he became a dresser and assisted William Lucas, a surgeon. Keats immersed himself in his work, both in the lecture hall and the dissecting room. At this time Keats also met Astley Cooper, a distinguished surgeon and Keats's professor of anatomy and physiology. Cooper was well-read with a taste for poetry and liberal politics.

Keats may very well have continued his career in medicine, especially as it gave him an opportunity to relieve suffering, but he was becoming lonely and he turned to books for solace. Poetry was Keats's escape, offering a transcendental release in which he could leave the bonds of earth to communicate with the spiritual world of immortality. Two young contemporary poets were his source of renewal: Byron and Chatterton. Keats's devotion to his medical studies began to waver as he once again turned to his true passion—poetry—while his training at Guy's Hospital served to intensify his interest in the hidden life of nature.

Poetry was not the only passion in his life. Keats had fallen hopelessly in love with Fanny Brawne in the fall of 1818. Though it was love at first sight, Keats was very troubled and anxious in his relationships with women, and at first he felt rebuffed by Fanny. However, during the Christmas holidays of 1818, Keats proclaimed his love to Fanny and learned that she reciprocated. Nevertheless, though they became engaged, they never married, for Keats's devotion to his poetry and his growing illness turned their romance into a constant torment. While he often felt jealous when Fanny went to dances without him, her health and vitality in contrast to his own illness was a source of even greater anguish. Perhaps his poem, "On Melancholy," expresses best his intensity of feeling: "She dwells with Beauty—Beauty that must die; / And Joy, whose hand is ever at his lips / Bidding adieu; and aching Pleasure nigh, / Turning to poison while the bee-mouth sips. . . ." When Keats set out for Italy in 1820, he would never again see Fanny, or his homeland.

Keats had stopped writing at the age of twenty-five, shortly before his death in Rome on February 23, 1821. A few months earlier, on October 21, 1820, Keats and his traveling companion, the young artist Joseph Severn, had just sailed into the Bay of Naples. Keats had long dreamed of visiting this city and his first view of the city, at sunrise, presented a dazzling landscape of white villas, terraced vineyards, and olive orchards set amid the hills of Campagna. But shortly thereafter, they learned that they would not be able to land for several days, because Keats and Severn had left London during an epidemic of typhus and would have to abide by the requisite six weeks of quarantine.

They had already spent a month at sea and when they were finally able to step ashore in a driving rain, some of the magic was dispelled by the crowd of beggars and ballad-singers, the pungent smell of fish, and the sight of children playing in the filthy gutters. But worst of all, Keats was suffering from the heartache of having left Fanny Brawne. Everything in his trunk reminded him of her, including the silk lining she had put in his cap. However, his spirits improved a little at the sight of the last grapes being harvested and the fragrance of late roses blooming in front of the cottages by the road.

Their stay in Naples was brief, and on November 8 Keats and Severn set out for Rome. The journey was arduous as they traveled in a small carriage over very bad roads, stopping at primitive villages where they were served vile food. Midpoint on their route, they entered the vast malarial wasteland of the Campagna. Nevertheless, Keats was anxious to get to Rome, where a young Scottish physician, Dr. James Clark, awaited his arrival. His new physician had already secured an apartment for them overlooking a piazza lined with the shops of print-sellers and artisans, flower vendors, and artists' models.

A warm-hearted doctor who took an interest in Keats's poetry, Clark's initial diagnosis of Keats unfortunately did not alert him to the severity of the poet's failing health. Indeed, for a brief time, Keats's health appeared to be improving as he began to discuss poetry once again. He even contemplated writing a long poem on the story of Sabrina, a river-nymph in Milton's *Comus*. But Keats knew that he could no longer conceal his illness, and in a letter to his friend, Charles Brown, he revealed his full knowledge that his end was near. He had already endured a series of debilitating hemorrhages and unending hunger from losing the ability to digest any food. "I have an habitual feeling of my real life having past, and that I am leading a posthumous existence," he said.

Keats was dying of consumption. In his last hours, he clung to Severn, making a courageous and valiant effort to console his young friend. "Don't be frightened—I shall die easy—be firm, and thank God it has come!" Although his life had been short, his literary achievements far exceeded that of Chaucer, Shakespeare, and Milton at the same age. ❀

Introduction
to the Ode

The ode is a genre of poetry that originated in ancient Greece. It was originally intended as a formal public address delivered during important state functions. Taken from the Greek word *aeidein*, which means to sing or chant, the ode is also a lyrical form of poetry, and, like its Hebrew and Egyptian analogues, it played an important role in religious practices. It is a complexly organized poem, intended for important state functions and ceremonies, such as a ruler's birthday, accession, funeral, or the unveiling of a public work. Thus, it is a mode of public address. Furthermore, its tone is emotional, exalted, and intense, incorporating whatever divine myths are appropriate to the occasion. The classical ode consists of regular stanzas—a strophe, an antistrophe, and an epode. The strophe is the initial component the Greek chorus chanted while moving from one side of the stage to another, followed by a metrically identical antistrophe that was chanted in accompaniment to a reverse movement, which finally lead up to the epode, sung by the chorus while standing still.

There are two basic types of odes, the Pindaric and the Horatian. The first type is based on the occasional odes written by Pindar (between 522–442 B.C.), which were designed for choric song and dance and intended to be performed in a Dionysiac theatre (or in the Agora to celebrate athletic victories). Pindar was patronized by the great aristocrats of his time, the ruling families of Cyrene, Syracuse, and Acragas, and in common with his contemporaries, he placed great value on athletic performance. Thus, the ode was intended to commemorate some of the highest human achievements, with the longer victory odes containing a small portion of a mythic narrative. Pindar most often chose myths dealing with the heroes of the victor's city and usually focused on a specific event or single incident, as audience familiarity was assumed, and often took a moral position within the context of the events being narrated. The formal structure of the Pindaric ode included an announcement of victory, praise for the champion, an invocation to the gods, and praise of the athlete's city and family. However, also incorporated within this celebratory poem were reminders of the victor's mortality, a prayer to ward off bad luck, an awareness of the pitfalls of vanity or the dangers of provoking envy in the gods, and the importance of inherent excellence.

The second basic type of classical ode is named for the Latin poet Horace (65–68 B.C.), for whom there exists a considerable amount of biographical information from Seutonius as well as Horace's allusions to his life in his own poetry. His father, a small landowner in Venusia and a *coactor* (public auctioneer), apparently had the means to send his son to Rome and then Athens, for what was the equivalent of an aristocratic education in his times. Though Horace served in the army of Brutus, Brutus ultimately fell and the family's property was lost. Horace, who considered himself lucky just to return to Italy, became a *scriba apparitores*, one of a group of salaried officials attending Roman magistrates and priests, a position that brought social prestige and the opportunity to meet such great poets as Virgil and Varius Rufus, who in turn introduced Horace to a circle of writers. When he was later given the famous Sabine farm, he was afforded the time and financial security to devote himself to writing poetry. In contrast to the odes of Pindar, the Horation ode is personal rather than public, general rather than occasional, tranquil rather than intense, and contemplative and philosophic in character, intended for a private reader in his library rather than a theatrical spectator. Horace declared that his main literary model in his *Odes* was that of early Greek poetry from Lesbos, the poetry of Alcaeus and Sappho. Nevertheless, he was trained in what was considered the "modern" contemporary Hellenistic style in which the simple language of early Greek models was transformed into a sophisticated and highly allusive style that reflected the complex literary world of Augustan Rome. Although Horace's themes are the usual ones to be found in ancient poetry, his treatment differs. For instance, his hymns to the gods are meant to explore the world of Greek divinity and the aesthetic pleasures it could provide rather than be an emphasis on pious worship; and in his treatment of love, Horace tries to free himself from extreme emotions, preferring a calm and cheerful stance. Likewise, friendship is an important theme throughout his odes, which are addressed to specific friends, offering them advice and assistance. Horace's influence on modern poetry is seen most pointedly in his sustained epigram, a form of writing that makes a satiric or concise observation, ranging in tone from sharp to gentle.

In Europe, the history of the ode begins with the Renaissance rediscovery of the classic forms. The Italian and French humanistic odes of the 15th and early 16th centuries adopted the ode's structure to explore new subject matters. In the English tradition, however, the ode became irregular, based on a structure of turn, counter-turn, and stand, a series of balanced opposites. The genre attained popularity in the 17th century with Abraham Cowley's *Pindarique Odes* in 1656, in which Cowley attempted to capture the spirit and tone of Pindar rather than a formal imitation of the classical poet. In the 18th century, the great formal odes began with John Dryden, in such works as "Ode for St. Cecilia's Day," a poem that celebrates both musical inspiration and devotion to the events surrounding the legendary martyrdom of St. Cecelia celebrated in *The Golden Legend*. Further on in the 18th century, the odes of Gray and Collins, employing a wide range of emotions such as anxiety and terror, used the ode to express a crisis, namely to thematize the tension between the modern lyric and the poems and genres of the past. In the 18th century the ode became the vehicle for expressing the sublime, lofty thoughts of intellectual and spiritual concerns, such as Shelley's "Ode to the West Wind," which combines many classical elements while at the same time vacillating between the external world and the world of the imagination. For the Romantic poets, the ode became the vehicle for expressing the sublime, lofty thoughts of intellectual and spiritual concerns; at the same time, it provided a vehicle for reasserting the power and preeminence of the poet's voice. As Paul Fry notes in his introductory chapter of *The Poet's Calling in the English Ode*, "Like the hymn, the ode or 'hymn extempore' longs for participating in the divine, but it never participates communally, never willing supplies a congregation with common prayer because it is bent on recovering a priestly role that is not pastoral but hermetic." He continues, "By imitating hymnody, however, an ode reveals *its* conception of a hymn as a being-present to a transcendent, originary voice."

For Keats, the ode was a vehicle to express his never-ending quest to transcend mortal time and thereby establish an absolute and inviolable permanence of human and poetic beauty. ❁

Thematic Analysis of
"Ode on a Grecian Urn"

Written in 1819 and published in 1820, "Ode on a Grecian Urn" is a detailed description of an urn, a vessel traditionally used for a variety of ceremonial purposes. The rhetorical procedure Keats used to describe the urn is known as *ekphrasis*. While the first appearance of the term ekphrasis occurs in the writings of Dionysius of Halicarnassus, it later became a school exercise, the objective of which was to create a picture so vivid that it would bring the subject or object before the eyes. However, it is only in modern times that ekphrasis was narrowly construed to the literary description of a work of art. The most famous of these modern descriptions is Keats's "Ode on a Grecian Urn."

The urn described in this poem is made of marble, a type of limestone, which is itself crystallized and unchangeable, the result of the natural processes of metamorphoses. Furthermore, this imaginary urn belongs to the classical tradition of the pastoral, a type of poem representing an idealized portrait of rustic life in an imaginary Golden Age, the central theme of which was the lives and loves of shepherds and shepherdesses. The intention of the pastoral poem varied, sometimes presenting romantic or sentimental views of life, lamenting the loss or death of a loved one, while at other times making a political or social statement. During the Renaissance, the pastoral was further developed into the elegy, or poem of mourning. The elegy included a statement of grief, an inquiry into the cause of death, the sympathy and weeping of Nature, a procession of mourners, and consolation and overcoming of grief in finding some higher purpose for the loss of the loved one. What is especially interesting is that Keats chose to write an ode *about* a Grecian urn, which immediately raises the question as to whom the speaker is addressing. Keats will rework all of these literary conventions for his own artistic purposes.

The **first stanza** of the poem sets forth many of the issues and tensions Keats will explore throughout the poem. From the very first line, the audience or listener is left with a puzzling statement as Keats addresses one of the figures on the urn as "Thou still unravish'd bride of quietness." It is left for the addressee to decide whether "still" is an adverb describing simply a moment in time in which a change is anticipated, or if "still" is a descriptive adjective denoting that the figure on the urn is stationary. At a still further remove from any identification with mortal existence, the "still unravish'd bride" is declared to be a "foster-child of silence and slow time." She has no genealogical connection with human life because she is, simply, a product of the poet's imagination, set forever within her marble domain, inhabiting an ideal space, among the pastoral "dales of Arcady," in which she is no longer subject to the ravages of time or the vagaries and unpredictability of sexual love. Keats's "still unravish'd bride" is exempt from the passions of mortal existence, even from the frenzied portrayal of "mad pursuit" that seemingly threatens to consume the other figures depicted on the urn. "What struggle to escape? / What pipes and timbrels? What wild ecstasy?" Perhaps the bride and all the other figures depicted on the urn can best be described as existing in a state of frozen animation, the perfect expression of Keats's longing for permanence in a world of change.

In the **second stanza**, another interesting transformation of the ode takes place when Keats celebrates the silent music that can only be implied—but never heard—by the portrayal of piping rustics. He goes so far as to say that the *potential* for music is far preferable than the actual music, the "sensual ear" in the everyday world of mortal existence. "Heard melodies are sweet, but those unheard / Are sweeter." The poet is deliberately elevating the unsung melodies that are "more endear'd"; they are made more valuable because they are more appropriate to a world of eternal youth preserved within this state of frozen animation. "Pipe to the spirit ditties of no tone: / Fair youth, beneath the trees, thou canst not leave / Thy song."

These ecstatic figures are spared the vagaries and unpredictability of sexual love, for their love is in a state of constant deferral, promised but never to be consummated. "Bold lover, never, never canst thou kiss / . . . yet do not grieve; / She cannot fade." And, thus, death is forever precluded from entering this marble paradise. Tennyson alludes to these same lines in his poem, "Locksley Hall," as the speaker states, "Better thou and I were lying, hidden from the heart's disgrace, / Roll'd in one another's arms, and silent in a last embrace." But for Keats, the lovers represented on the urn are in a state of arrested animation, and because they are unable to act upon their feelings, they seemingly have the ability to hold on to their hope forever. "Bold lover, never, never canst thou kiss, / Though winning near the goal—yet do not grieve: / She cannot fade, though thou hast not thy bliss, / For ever wilt thou love, and she be fair." Though Keats's lovers are far beyond the grip of time and human interference, we are made to feel that any attempt to consummate their love will prove to be immediately fatal. In a word, their love is absolutely impossible.

In the **third stanza**, Keats further expounds on the virtues of his highly wrought, imaginative world in which the melodist never tires, which Nature's endless cycle of death and renewal can never touch. "Ah, happy, happy boughs! That cannot shed / Your leaves, nor ever bid the spring adieu." This is a world in which the lovers are spared the pain of growing old and are safe from the grief that accompanies the excess of mortal passions. "For ever panting, and for ever young; / All breathing human passion far above, / That leaves a heart high-sorrowful and cloy'd." Yet, the absolute bliss of this ideal world is deceptive; the bliss lies only on the surface, for though Keats tells us that the lovers are exempt from experiencing the ravages of time, the excessive happiness expressed a few lines before ("More happy love! more happy, happy love! / For ever warm and still to be enjoy'd") is in the final analysis unstable, bringing us closer to mortal experience. The urn's unconditional happiness seems to be as cloyed, surfeited, and as overly abundant as the world which it denies. The ominous note on which the third stanza concludes—with a "burning forehead, and a parching tongue"—will become increasing intensified.

Indeed, in the **fourth stanza**, the pastoral scene has now been transformed into a frightening landscape in which a terrible price must be paid in exchange for absolute happiness and contentment. "Who are these coming to the sacrifice? / To what green altar, O mysterious priest, / Lead'st thou that heifer lowing at the skies, / And all her silken flanks with garlands drest?" The pastoral peace and quiet has suddenly, and without warning, become an eerie landscape in which all traces of life will not only be destroyed but erased forever from memory, as if they never existed. "And, little town, thy streets for evermore / Will silent be; and not a soul to tell / Why thou art desolate, can e'er return."

So persuasive has Keats's portrayal been that we forget he is using a rhetorical device. He has succeeded so well in bringing his picture of the urn before our eyes that in the process he has seduced us into believing these figures actually exist. However, Keats's joyful society exists only on the urn—and that urn exists only in the poet's imagination.

In the **fifth stanza**, which concludes "Ode on a Grecian Urn," the poem confesses to being a brilliant and beautiful fiction. The stanza begins with Keats turning his attention to the urn and addressing it directly as an object of art, admitting to its luxurious and excessive sensuality. "O Attic shape! Fair attitude! with brede / Of marble men and maidens overwrought." Keats's use of the word *brede* (a poetic commonplace in the 17th and 18th centuries for anything interwoven and intricately embroidered) is also significant within the context of the poet's admission that he has reworked a wide variety of literary devices. In having brought the urn to life before our very eyes, he confesses that we have all been lead astray in entering into its idyllic world, equally deceived in our wish for eternal youth and beauty. "Thou, silent form, dost tease us out of thought / As doth eternity."

Having returned to the mortal world, realizing that we are merely gazing upon an alluring work of art, we see that the simple and appealing rustic landscape in which we have all but participated rightfully belongs to the marble as the only condition of its existence. "Cold Pastoral! / when old age shall this generation waste, / Thou shalt remain." The last lines—"Beauty is truth, truth beauty"—have been the subject of much critical debate ranging from the nonsensical to the ability of art to transform everything disagreeable; these lines are also a statement of the seduction to which we willingly succumb when gazing on a beautiful work of art. ❀

Critical Views on
"Ode on a Grecian Urn"

THOMAS H. SCHMID ON KEATS'S POETIC CONCERNS

[Thomas H. Schmid is the author of *Humor and Transgression in Peacock, Shelley and Byron: A Cold Carnival* (1992). In the excerpt below from his article, "Silence and Celebration: Pastoral Dialogism in Keats's 'Ode on a Grecian Urn,'" Schmid discusses the ways in which the poem reflects Keats's conflicting concerns—that is creating lofty poetry while at the same time achieving popularity with mass audiences.]

In a letter to his publisher in the summer of 1819 Keats worries over the question of his literary popularity in terms that have become commonplace to Keats scholars: "I feel every confidence that if I choose I may be a popular writer," Keats writes; "that I will never be; but for all that I will get a livelihood—I equally dislike the favour of the public with the love of a woman—they are both a cloying treacle to the wings of independence." Recent commentaries have elucidated Keats's anxiety over the kind of readership that he feels would secure his popularity at the cost of his art, and even of his masculinity, pointing particularly to Keats's association of female readers with a debased literary class he repeatedly "disdains," as Margaret Homans says, "to court." ⟨. . .⟩

The issue of Keats's fears, especially in 1819, concerning both "highbrow" and "lowbrow" audiences of *any* gender bears relevance to what is usually regarded as one of his more "highbrow" lyrics, "Ode on a Grecian Urn." Despite the speaker's tone of lofty aestheticism at the conclusion of the ode, the poem itself comprises a dialogue inhabited by Keats's conflicting desires for, on the one hand, a literary popularity that would betoken his ability to be heard by mass audiences, and, on the other, a literary immortality that would transcend the particular material conditions of contemporary popularity and grant his poetry the same privileged status of the "museum" artifact that the ode gives the urn: the status of "anthologized art."

Latent within the frozen scene of the urn, itself an image of pastoral timelessness and a "Golden Age" that transcends history, is nevertheless the suggestion of a cultural dialogue, one based on *communitas*, collective ritual, and popular art forms such as the piper's music. This is the dialogue the speaker seemingly wishes to reopen at the beginning of the ode, but it is one that by definition cannot exist on the same (a) temporal plane as the monologized, lyric voice of "immortal" art. To become "high" art the piper's song must be silenced, its historical particularity traded in for some expression of immortal universality. In consequence, it will no longer be "heard," at least with any kind of immediacy (the immediacy for which Keats himself, as I discuss below, devoutly wished). The speaker of the ode both desires and seeks to deny the dialogue with the "low" (popular) discourses represented by the piper and the various scenes of communal sacrifice and celebration on the urn, which he interrogates at the beginning of the poem. Ultimately he chooses denial, opting to aestheticize the urn and its decorations in a monologic statement about a "universal" beauty and truth that transcend temporal popularity. The rhetorical drama of the ode itself, however, challenges the speaker's conclusions in a way that reflects Keats's own ambivalence about the conflicting ends of "high" and "low" art, of popular and refined discourse, of simple and complex expression.

Certainly "low" art is not without its attractions for Keats, and throughout 1819 he tends to register a certain defensiveness and disgust over his apparent exile from educated literary culture, writing to Haydon in March, for instance, that he "will not mix with that most vulgar of all crowds the literary," and to the George Keatses in September that "my name with the literary fashionables is vulgar—I am a weaver boy to them": two expressions that not only ironically displace the charge of vulgarism from the literary crowd to himself, but also temporally frame the probable writing of the "Grecian Urn" in May. Furthermore, Keats is indeed repeatedly attracted by some hazy vision of himself as a popular writer, one who would be willing to write just about anything "on the liberal side of the question, for whoever will pay," though his ambivalence remains: "I feel it in my power to become a popular writer," he admits to Reynolds in August—"I feel it in my strength to refuse the poisonous suffrage of a public."

To be popular or to be "literary": that is Keats's 1819 question, and both courses seem to him, at alternate times, vulgar. The Roman *vulgus* was, of course, the crowd, the common-people, and Keats's seemingly contradictory statements about which "crowd" is vulgar— the common crowd of laborers metonymically evoked by the epithet "weaver boy," or the necessarily exclusive crowd of the consciously "literary"—suggest a collapsing of the very distinctions by which educated (middle and upper class) Regency literary society separates itself from the crowd. To say that there is no more vulgar crowd than the literary is to draw attention to the transparency of its motives, to the ordinary material conditions that make its exclusiveness possible. The literary crowd is in fact never more "common" than in its claims to uniqueness, to thinking and feeling differently from the "crowd," and to an expressiveness of particular artistic value. ⟨. . .⟩

—Thomas H. Schmid, "Silence and Celebration: Pastoral Dialogism in Keats's 'Ode on a Grecian Urn,'" *Keats-Shelley Journal* 44 (1995): pp. 66–69.

⊚

Thomas C. Kennedy on the Tension between Poem and Work of Art

[Thomas C. Kennedy is the author of "Rhetoric and Meaning in the House of Fame" (1996) and "From Anna Barbauld's Hymns in Prose to William Blakes's 'Songs of Innocence and Experience'" (1998). In the excerpt below from his article, "Platonism in Keats's 'Ode on a Grecian Urn,'" Kennedy discusses the creative process that allows us to experience, simultaneously, the creation of two works of art, a real poem and an imaginary urn, and the philosophical tensions that surface between the two.]

The 22 November 1817 letter to Bailey involved, as we have seen, an inherent contradiction: an assertion of the supremacy of imagination over reason by means of a rational argument. Keats continued the argument in his poetry, a medium in which imagination could directly demonstrate its supremacy. The special value that Diotima places on artistic creativity is particularly explicit in Keats's poems describing works of art, especially Greek works of art, like the sonnet "On Seeing the Elgin Mables" and the "Ode on a Grecian Urn."

In both the sonnet and the ode, Keats chose to write in a dramatic rather than in a narrative mode. That is to say, Keats did not write in the past tense about having seen a work of art as he wrote, for example, in the past tense about having read Chapman's translation in "On First Looking into Chapman's Homer." Instead, Keats wrote in the present tense as if he were in the immediate presence of the sculpture or the urn. The effect of this choice is that in both poems the fictional action of the poem seems to be the genesis of the poem itself. As Philip Fisher points out in "A Museum with One Work Inside: Keats and the Finality of Art," we seem to be witnessing the process by which the meditations of a poet in the presence of a work of art take the form of a poem. Thus the poet demonstrates rather than talks about imagination.

In the sonnet, the Elgin marbles represent the Platonic ideal. Keats uses a traditional rhetorical device, description by negation, describing the work of art by describing his inability to describe it. The effect is to place the ideal beyond the limits of human experience.

Although both the ode and sonnet employ the same fiction of the dramatic mode, there is an important contrast between the contexts in which the ode and sonnet were written. In the sonnet, Keats seems to assume that his reader is familiar with specific works of art, the Elgin Marbles, and therefore the poet is free to focus not on these ancient reliefs but on his own feelings, his own limitations. This focus on the poet's response is not possible in the "Ode on a Grecian Urn" for, as Sidney Colvin discovered after careful research, the famous urn is an imaginary urn. Therefore, the poet must, through his detailed description, create the urn for us in the poem. Thus, the subject matter of the "Ode on a Grecian Urn" is not, strictly speaking, a work of art but rather the creating of works of art. We witness the simultaneous creation of two works of art: the imaginary genesis of a real poem and the real genesis of an imaginary urn. The Platonic ideal is thus further removed from the material world by being an imagined rather than material object. The energy of the ode derives in part from a *philosophical* tension, a

Platonic tension, between the subject and the poem, between the imagined urn and the real ode.

In creating an imaginary urn that speaks, Keats was continuing a year and a half later the dialogue between poet and philosopher in the 22 November letter to Bailey. In choosing the dramatic mode, however, Keats chose not to *argue* for the power of the imagination (a contradiction in the letter), but rather to *demonstrate* the power of the imagination. There is also a similarity between Keats's relation to the imagined urn and Socrates' relation to Diotima: just as we recognize in the voice of Diotima Socrates talking to himself, in the same way, the voice of the urn is the voice of the poet separated from himself, the poet reflected.

A second influence on the ode from Diotima's speech in the *Symposium* is more specific. Diotima defines love as neither human nor divine, but: "intermediate . . . between the mortal and the immortal." Keats echoes this definition in his question, "What men or gods are these?" These figures on the urn, as representations of *eros,* are to the poet indeterminant between the human and the divine in keeping with Diotima's definiton. The uncertainty and questions of Socrates responding to Diotima's definition correspond to the uncertainty and questions of the poet facing the urn. ⟨. . .⟩

Permanence and change are represented in the ode by the urn and the poet's words. The urn represents that "which is always real being," while the poet's language represents that which "consists in a state of becoming to be." Keats's creation of an imaginary urn thus corresponds to the creation of the universe as described in the *Timaeus*: the permanent idea, the imaginary urn, gives a form to impermanent matter, the poet's language. A real urn would of course be subject to physical change, but the antiquity and stasis of the work of art suggest by their relative permanence those values which in Platonism are not subject to change. It is these permanent values, not antiquity or stasis, which according to the passage from the *Timaeus*, in so far as they serve as the "paradigm" for the work of art's creation, account for its beauty.

—Thomas C. Kennedy, "Platonism in Keats's 'Ode on a Grecian Urn,'" *Philological Quarterly* 75, no. 1 (Winter 1996): pp. 92–95.

[Jason Mauro is the author of *Huck Finn and the Post-Nuclear Age: Lighting Out for the New Frontier* (1997). In the excerpt below from his article, "The Shape of Despair: Structure and Vision in Keats's 'Ode on a Grecian Urn,'" Mauro discusses the idea of audience participation in the act of reading the poem.]

With sympathetic eyes Karl Kroeber sees Keats as a Western poet "dying of poetry," withering in the arid gap between the audience he had achieved and the community he longed for. According to Kroeber, Keats's particular despair outlines the limits of all Western poetry, whose domain, in Stuart M. Sperry's terms, is the "dream" rather than the "vision." By comparing the dynamics of Keats's "Fall of Hyperion" to the Ojibwa "Deer Dancing Song," Kroeber claims that Keats was doomed by the traditions of Western poetry to the isolating activity of reporting dream material to an audience rather than transferring a visionary experience to a community:

> There was for [Keats], as for all Western poets, no social outlet through which to discharge the dangerous potency within his psyche. Publication, admiring friends, even wide popularity are not effective substitutes for the Indian's tribe. The tribe consists not in listeners or audience merely, but of cultural supporters who can physically aid the poet by giving a social form to the power speaking through him.

The tribe, as distinct from the audience, reproduces the dream, enacting it rather than merely admiring, reiterating, or critiquing it. According to Kroeber, the Ojibwa singer transfers "energy," a vision, to the tribe and thus forms a community, whereas Keats is doomed to draw energy and applause from his audience. The louder he shouts out the content of his dream, the more isolated he becomes.

I wonder though if the "Ode on a Grecian Urn" both encourages and provides a location for the kind of enactment that Kroeber reserves for non-Western poetry like the Ojibwa "Deer Dancing Song." I would like to suggest that Keats's ode is a site for a ritual transformation of the reader, where we are allowed to participate in a transformative vision rather than witness a poet's dream. The act of reading the poem is, I believe, energy producing rather than energy consuming (using Kroeber's terms), and I am encouraged to put the poem down after having read it rather than to critique or fetishize it. Of course, the act of writing this critique contradicts this assertion, but I wonder then if it is the traditions and necessities of Western criticism that delineate the breach between audience and community. I had the opportunity to teach this poem to a class called "Inventing Death," which was designed to investigate cross-cultural attitudes toward death and dying. Many of my dying students found this poem to be, to say the least, useful and transformative. The "Ode on a Grecian Urn," then, stands perhaps as an antidote to Kroeber's lament that "it is not easy to find any Western art that doesn't serve as a locus for collecting power to itself rather than passing it on into socially productive activity." ⟨...⟩

Even the gesture, common in the criticism, of ascribing a geometric shape to the ode speaks to me of a participatory gesture, tracing a shape with a finger, placing a hand in a handprint. Helen Vendler presents a schematic of the poem's structural form, a triple "parabolic trajectory," with each curve representing the rise of the poet's aesthetic reverie and that reverie's eventual fall, brought about by the inexorable "fact of process." Vendler holds that the fundamental outline of the poem "is that of a poet coming, in woe, to a work of art, interrogating it, and being solaced by it." The poet's initial woe is generated by "the transience of life itself," and, she argues, the urn serves as an antidote to that troubling transience. ⟨...⟩

The shape I find most descriptive of the radically transformative nature of the ode, however, is neither a circle nor a series of parabolas. More accurately, the ode inscribes a sine-wave, with five distinctive points along its length: first, the poet is steeped in despair brought about by the world's unrelenting flux; second, upon encountering the urn, he is filled with the hope that he has found an antidote to his despair; third, he finds that his hope is unfounded, that the antidote was no more than a placebo; fourth, as he more closely examines the urn, he finds that it embodies a terror far more intense than the despair from which he originally sought relief, that the placebo is in fact a poison; and finally, he embraces the transient condition of the world as an antidote to the terror inherent in the urn. The most distinguishing feature of the sine-wave, as distinct from a circle or a series of parabolas, is that the point of origin—the poet's initial despair *from* which he wishes to ascend—becomes the point of salvation *to* which, by the end of the ode, he wishes to climb.

> —Jason Mauro, "The Shape of Despair: Structure and Vision in Keats's 'Ode on a Grecian Urn,'" *Nineteenth-Century Literature* 52, no. 3 (December 1997): pp. 289–291.

⊛

GERALDINE FRIEDMAN ON THE RELATIONSHIPS BETWEEN SPEAKER, READER, AND TEXT

[Geraldine Friedman is the author of *The Insistence of History: Revolution in Burke, Wordsworth, Keats and Baudelaire* (1996). In the excerpt below from her article, "The Erotics of Interpretation in Keats's 'Ode on a Grecian Urn': Pursuing the Feminine," Friedman discusses the eroticism of the scenes depicted on the urn as signaling highly "charged relationships *between* the speaker and the urn, and *between* the reader and the text."]

If on the level of plot, "Ode on a Grecian Urn" dramatizes a mind struggling to grasp an object, the poem's seemingly discreet title suggests a deeper conflict in textual strategy. On the one hand, as an ode, the poem announces its functioning as a figure and a fiction: an extended direct address to an entity incapable of literal response. On the other hand, as an ode *on*, "Grecian Urn" foregrounds its material condition as writing on a surface. Between these contradictory emphases on the sounding of voice and the silence of inscription opens a gap in which the poem stages an eroticized drama of interpretation. Structured as a double analogy, the text suggests that the erotic scenes *on* the urn figure the charged relationships both *between* the speaker and the urn, and *between* the reader and the text.

This circulation of desire begins on the first panel of the urn's frieze, which is explored in the first strophe of the poem:

What leaf-fring'd legend haunts about thy shape
Of deities or mortals, or of both.
In Tempe or the dales of Arcady?

What men or gods are these? What maidens loth?
What mad pursuit? What struggle to escape?
What pipes and timbrels? What wild ecstasy?

As the first of several erotic scenes, this orgiastic pursuit is framed
from the beginning by the speaker's desire to know the urn.
Similarly, in our frustrated attempts to understand an attractive but
elusive poem, we, as readers, re-enact the speaker's sexual urgency
as he tries to penetrate the mysteries of the "still unravish'd bride
of quietness." Here, interpretative activity, both inside the text and
between the text and the reader, is driven by an eros of questioning,
represented on the object of interpretation itself. It could be
said that the speaker's eagerness to read the "leaf-fring'd legend"
en-genders a story about gender, where interpretation is figured as a
male subject's sexual pursuit of a female object of desire. This essay
will show that the ode's textual strategy turns inevitably into a
sexual tragedy in which the reader, forced to occupy the position of
the speaker, is complicit. "Ode on a Grecian Urn" thus represents its
own model of reading as a structurally gendered process, and, in
this respect, it has deep affinities with the self-representations of the
hermeneutic tradition.

In depicting the acquisition of knowledge as a classic love story
with a seemingly familiar plot and characters, the text dramatizes a
key figure in hermeneutics, the figure of interpretation as erotic
conversation. Hans-Georg Gadamer, who perhaps makes this aspect
of the tradition most explicit, takes dialogue as the quintessential
hermeneutical situation: ". . . hermeneutical conversation . . .
coincides with the very act of understanding," he asserts in *Truth
and Method*. In aesthetic experience, the art object becomes for
Gadamer an interlocutor on the level of a human subject; the work
of art "says something" and as such "is like a person." The ideal
interpretative situation is the interpersonal one of "true
conversation," where the self opens itself to the other and respects
the other's point of view. Thus Gadamer illustrates the
hermeneutical problem as "lovers talking to each other," a situation
that suggests privileged access between two selves. ⟨. . .⟩

From its very first line, the poetic text is forced to work out the
dark consequences of a figural logic that Gadamer wilfully ignores,
the figural logic that marries the aesthetic and the erotic in the form
of a conversation.

To approach the poem through its address is to read in the gaps of the secondary literature, which has largely ignored the text's figurative moment to concentrate instead on its descriptive one. In so far as the text describes, it is structured by a set of symmetrical oppositions: the visual versus the verbal, the spatial versus the temporal, the real versus the ideal, and the ephemerality of the human condition versus the permanence of art. The eminence of these categories in the ode has produced a long line of interpretations in the ekphrastic tradition of *ut pictura poesis*. Yet, if the ode does paint a picture, that picture is contained by and remains secondary to the direct address that constitutes the ode as a lyric genre. What is really at stake is the figure of voice that subsumes the poem's thematic polarities and generates a story dependent on the somewhat different relation between masculinity and femininity; the erotic drama of interpretation is made possible by the personifying address in the first place. Thus, against the accumulated historical weight of interpretation, this essay will displace the representational aspect of the ode to privilege its rhetoric.

The poem, then, creates the fiction of an intersubjective reciprocity between urn and speaker, and between text and reader, a reciprocity that attributes to both the urn and the ode the ability to hear and answer, and thus also understand, the questions put to them.

—Geraldine Friedman, "The Erotics of Interpretation in Keats's 'Ode on a Grecian Urn': Pursuing the Feminine," *Studies in Romanticism* 32, no. 2 (Summer 1993): pp. 225–229.

ADAM ROBERTS ON THE IMAGINATIVE URN

[Adam Roberts is the author of *Robert Browning Revisited* (1996) and *Romantic and Victorian Long Poems: A Guide* (1999). In the excerpt below from his article, "Keats's 'Attic Shape': 'Ode on a Grecian Urn' and Non-Euclidian Geometry," Roberts focuses on the nature of the imaginative urn and its ability to define the space which it inhabits.]

Here is a rather old-fashioned question with regard to Keats's 'Ode on a Grecian Urn': which urn, if any, did Keats have in mind when writing his poem? Was there (as many older Keats critics believed, exhausting themselves in the search for a possible single original) one particular urn? Or are we to believe Ian Jack's widely-endorsed opinion that the urn described by the poem is a sort of composite creation, made up of elements from various Greek *Objets d'art*? ⟨...⟩

Yet all these queries seem to beg a more basic question, a question that can be rather crudely framed as follows: in what sense can Keats's poem be said to be urn-shaped? Does the poem in any sense reproduce the contours of the urn it concerns? Perhaps such a question seems ill-advised. It is certainly possible to imagine an urn upon which is fashioned an illustration of the sort of scene Keats describes—leafy foliage above, grass below, and a procession of figures around the curve of the vase, beginning with men and maidens engaged in erotic struggles and (swivelling the urn before our eyes) moving on to a sacrifice at an altar. The details of the scene may be derived from various ancient Greek artifacts rather than any single urn, but this (it might be argued) does not alter the effect of the work. That such a mental picture can be derived from the poem is reflected in the unspoken assumption made by so many critics that the poem is based on a particular urn, one it is worth seeking out. The urn mentioned in the first stanza of 'Ode on Indolence' possesses exactly this circularity of design; and there the narrator specifically turns the shape for us.

> They passed like figures on a marble urn,
> When shifted round to see the other side;
> They came again; as when the urn once more
> Is shifted round, the first seen shades return;

The close relationship between the 'Ode on Indolence' and 'Ode on a Grecian Urn' has been commented upon by critics: Miriam Allot, for instance, discerns an 'obvious' link between the poems, which in turn might suggest a particular, urn-shaped provenance for the two poems.

But this is not necessarily the case. It is worth bearing in mind, elementary though the point is, that an urn, or a vase, belongs to a very particular class of artifacts. It, like a globe (or its topographical equivalents—a rugby ball, a pear), or a wedding-ring (or any 'ring doughnut' shape), but unlike most other forms of art, exhibits non-

Euclidian properties. This is not simply a question of existing in three-dimensions where a painting (say) exists in two; architecture exists in three dimensions, and yet can be readily comprehended in Euclidian terms (architect's plans, for instance). The difference in a torus is that any design placed upon it will be contiguous, it will lack a moment of defined origin, and a moment of defined termination. An urn is a particular form of torus, one that defines a certain space: in addition to contiguity it brings with it an awareness of the difference between 'inside' and 'outside' the artifact—the urn surrounds a certain three-dimensional area. If this artistic space, represented by an urn, is contrasted with other artifacts the difference becomes clearer. A two-dimensional work of art—a painting, say, or the Shield of Achilles—lends itself to linear, teleological expression. It may embody circularised patterns, but these must be comprehended within the frames of the artifact. Other, more necessarily linear forms of art (a poem, or the song of the nightingale) are more obviously noncontiguous; they begin at a certain moment. There is a time before which the nightingale is not singing, and there is a time after which it is singing no longer. When Keats chooses the self-reflexive strategy of creating works of art about works of art, the artifacts he opts for are frequently linear in this way—the nightingale's song, the stained-glass window in *The Eve of St. Agnes*, the literary sonnets to Spenser or Chapman. ⟨. . .⟩

If we turn to the 'Ode', it is difficult to avoid the sense that the urn Keats elaborates is a curiously flat, Euclidian urn: a non-contiguous, non-toroid urn. Indeed, it could be argued that an 'ode' about a torus is an oxymoron to begin with: the dialectic progression implicit in strophe, antistrophe and epode suggests development, such that the position reached at the end of the poem is in some sense different (albeit derived) from the beginning. This is not really compatible with the nature of a torus. It could certainly be argued that the details of 'Ode on a Grecian Urn' undercut any idea of toroidity.

Hollowness is, for instance, a necessary aspect of an urn. Vases can be storage jars; they might be full of wine, or might (as with Isabella's pot) contain precious objects, the objects themselves then likely to become the focus of attention. We might, just as well, be dealing with a funerary urn, storing the ashes of the dead. So a logical question is—what does the Grecian urn contain? Or, importantly, do we get a sense of the urn as a shape that *can* contain things? It is, as the opening styles it, a 'still unravished bride': the analogy seems to be with a woman, such that the interior of the urn is comparable to the womb. To what degree does this analogy bear up under examination? And what is made of the analogy in the rest of the poem? The answer to the second question—nothing—has a bearing on the first, since the various associations of the 'interior-womb' analogy—future fertility, humanity, the way in which inward organs (consumptive lungs, perhaps, as much as wombs) affect outward health—are quite *at odds with* the burden of the ode as a whole. They belong to the realm of 'human passion' from which the urn is distinctly and absolutely separate. The relationship between inner and outer, indeed, is a painful one as far as humans are concerned—the heart (in the breast) is high sorrowful, the tongue (in the mouth) is parched, the head is an arena for headaches.

> All breathing human passion far above,
>   That leaves a heart high sorrowful and cloyed,
>   A burning forehead, and a parching tongue.

—Adam Roberts, "Keats's 'Attic Shape': 'Ode on a Grecian Urn' and Non-Euclidian Geometry," *Keats-Shelley Review*, no. 9 (Spring 1995): pp. 1–3, 5–6.

ꙮ

AILEEN WARD ON THE RELATIONSHIP BETWEEN THE VISUAL ARTS AND POETRY

[Aileen Ward is the author of *The Unfurling of Entity: Metaphor in Poetic Theory* (1987) and editor of *Confessions of an English Opium Eater and Other Writings* (1985). In the excerpt below from her book, *John Keats: The Making of a Poet*, Ward discusses the biographical context for the composition of "Ode on a Grecian Urn," focusing on Keats's interest in the relationship between the visual arts and poetry.]

Keats copied the "Ode to Psyche" out in his journal just before closing it on May 3 and hurrying off to Walthamstow to collect his sister's letter to George. One of Birkbeck's sons was leaving for Illinois shortly and would carry their letters direct. As he jumbled the sheets together, Keats's eye was evidently caught by his description of the daydream he had had one lazy morning in March. "Neither Poetry, nor Ambition, nor Love have any alertness of countenance as they pass by me," he had written; "they seem rather like three figures on a greek vase—a Man and two women—whom no one but myself could distinguish in their disguisement." The image struck him as he looked at it again, and he tried working it out in another ode. The result, the "Ode on Indolence," was not a success. His original idea had cooled for almost two months and could no longer give vital shape to the poem or significance to the allegorical figures, who merely appear and reappear in a vain effort to rouse him from his daydreaming; and the conclusion, in which he dismisses Love and Poetry as well as Ambition, seems to ring false to his change of mood in the interval. Still the image haunted him, and he tried working it into another poem. When the vision first came to him in March, the immobility of the three figures had seemed a kind of reproach, an image of the paralysis which had overtaken the three central impulses of his life; in the first ode he tried, he was still separated from the figures—now slowly moving, but with averted glance—by his own determined indolence. Now, in the "Ode on a Grecian Urn," they are quickened into new life as Keats the perceiver becomes one with the thing perceived. As he questions the figures on the urn and seeks to enter into their existence, allegory becomes symbol and the vase takes on a meaning of its own—the relation between the imagination and its creations, the illusions and realities of art and life together.

The ode begins with a topic which Keats had debated many times at Hunt's and Haydon's, the contrast between the visual arts and poetry. In one of his most extraordinary metaphors—"Thou still unravish'd bride of quietness"—Keats invokes not only the immortal freshness of all great art, but also the enigmatic silence of the urn, which still can tell its tale "more sweetly than our rhyme," and the serenity it preserves amid the scene of Bacchic frenzy it depicts. These antinomies at once suggest another paradoxical aspect of pictorial art, its representation of movement through action arrested at its most dynamic moment. As the bride of quietness reaches the fullness of her beauty while "still unravish'd," the bold lover is most passionate while "winning near the goal." At first the poet finds the unenacted desire of the youth on the urn an incompletion, for which he must console him:

> do not grieve;
> She cannot fade, though thou hast not thy bliss,
> For ever wilt thou love, and she be fair!

Immediately he realizes that by this very arrest of impulse the lovers achieve a perfect bliss, "All breathing human passion far above," which escapes the satiety implicit in all fulfilment. Yet even this unchanging perfection of art—that of the unwearied melodist "for ever piping songs for ever new"—is realized, paradoxically, for only a brief moment. In the fourth stanza, as the poet turns to another scene, the eternity becomes a desolation. As his wondering imagination follows the procession to the woodland altar, it suddenly calls up the town they have forever deserted, its streets forever silent; the beauty immortalized at one point now implies an emptiness perpetuated at some other. At the farthest limits of this timeless world of art—that

> little town by river or sea shore,
> Or mountain-built with peaceful citadel . . .

which is not even represented on the urn—his enraptured contemplation is suddenly chilled by this discovery of the antinomies of experience. The timeless perfection of art, he now sees, contains its own imperfection, its immortality is in fact lifelessness—just as truly as the converse that joy may be won in the world of time only at the cost of the sorrow which time also brings in its revolutions. With this insight, the illusion of the urn's vital existence begins to collapse. The vase is only a vase, he remembers at last—a shape, an attitude, a form empty of meaning till the imagination fills it; and the human imagination cannot rest even in a dream of endless bliss. But at this moment, as he turns wearily back to the world of time, the urn breaks its silence with a message of consolation for him:

> Beauty is Truth,—Truth Beauty,—that is all
> Ye know on earth, and all ye need to know.

With this dramatic reversal of the dialogue, the illusory nature of the poet's own quest is finally revealed. He began by seeking in the world of art that perfect happiness and unshadowed beauty which Keats had long before rejected as a goal of life; and in exploring this world he finds in the end the joy and sorrow, the "light and shade" together that make up the world of actual experience. So at last he is ready to hear the enigmatic message of the urn and understand it for the first time. The imaginary world of art and the real world of experience, which he tried at first to disjoin, are in fact complementary and necessary to each other, for each serves to reveal the value of the other. If the real or "true" world is viewed as intensely and disinterestedly as the poet contemplates the imaginary world of the urn, it yields up its own beauty; if the beauty of art is searched to the very depths of speculation, truth will be found there. ⟨. . .⟩

—Aileen Ward, *John Keats: The Making of a Poet* (New York: Farrar, Straus and Giroux, 1986): pp. 280–282.

⊗

Thematic Analysis of
"The Eve of St. Agnes"

Written between January 18 and February 2, 1819, Keats's embellished account of the rites of St. Agnes's Eve is mainly taken from oral tradition, as well as additional information from Henry Ellis's 1813 edition of John Brand's *Observations on Popular Antiquities* (originally published in 1777). While various legends exist concerning St. Agnes's martyrdom, in Brand's account she was "a Roman virgin and martyr, who suffered in the tenth persecution under the Emperor Dioclesian A.D. 306. She was condemned to be debauched in the common stews before her execution, but her virginity was miraculously preserved by lightning and thunder from Heaven." The feast of St. Agnes is celebrated annually on January 21 in the basilica of St. Agnes by the presentation and blessing at the altar of two white unshorn lambs. Brand's account further records that, on the eve of St. Agnes's day, "many kinds of divination are practiced by virgins to discover their future husbands." Keats combined the superstitious belief in this practice with *Romeo and Juliet* (another important source for "The Eve of St. Agnes," given its theme of young love thwarted by feuding families). Keats weaves an elaborate narrative based on these and other literary sources, combining the legend of a saint with tales of ill-fated love, to tell a story of physical love that survives both death-dealing spirituality and unbridled profligacy.

The entire poem consists of a series of oppositions that stem from these two main conflicting ideas: spirituality that will not tolerate physical love and overindulgent and thoughtless licentiousness that will forever remain just that. These two conflicting themes become the outer framework of Keats's narrative, with the story of the lovers' determination to overcome these destructive forces contained within the middle sections of the poem.

As the poem begins, we are given a cold and dispirited portrayal of the landscape and inhabitants of this strange and alienating world. Nature itself seems to have forsaken her charges and left the animals of the field and forest without the resources to stay alive. "The owl, for all his feathers, was a-cold; / The hare limped trembling through the frozen grass, / And silent was the flock in woolly fold."

Neither can the Beadsman, a pensioner endowed to pray for the repose of his benefactor's family and friends, be long for the physical world; in the performance of his religious offices, he must absolutely deny this world. "Numb were the Beadsman's fingers, while he told / His rosary, and while his frosted breath, / Like pious incense from a censer old, / Seemed taking flight for heaven, without a death." The "meagre, barefoot, wan" Beadsman was never truly alive, we sense, and because of this, he will skip the necessary step of first dying in the natural world before entry into the spiritual realm. Indeed, the attenuated figure of the Beadsman seems at one with the cold and silent stone carvings that surround him. "The sculptured dead, on each side, seem to freeze, / Imprisoned in black, purgatorial rails. / Knights, ladies, praying in dumb ora'tries, He passeth by; and his weak spirit fails."

While this holy man sleeps among "rough ashes," a great riot is heard in another part of this "mansion foul," an "argent revelry" with images of a noisy crowd in aimless celebration, the fires are in sharp contrast with the Beadsman's frosty surroundings. "The silver, snarling trumpets 'gan to chide; / The level chambers, ready with their pride, / Were glowing to receive a thousand guests." These guests, thoughtlessly given over to an overindulged and unrestrained sensuality, are just as attenuated as the Beadsman. They are but figments of the imagination, living out a sensuous fiction, namely the romantic tales of a literary world long gone. "Numerous as shadows haunting fairily / The brain, new stuffed in youth, with triumphs gay / Of old romance. These let us wish away."

In his rejection of the old romances that affirm a lush sensuality, contrasted with a piousness that would assure a far greater life in the next world, Keats is implying a radically different agenda than that found in the romantic tales of a bygone age in which love so often went unrequited. Indeed, Madeline herself is at first seduced by these very same romantic tales, "asleep in lap of legends old," and must be awakened from these fictions in order for her love to be consummated. As will be seen by the end of "The Eve of St. Agnes," Keats affirms physical love in a world that seeks to undermine and destroy it; in this affirmation, the only chance for survival will be to escape its deadly message.

Keats's agenda is most fully realized in those sections of the poem (Stanzas 29 through 35) in which the lovers meet and proclaim their love. Agnes is the figure that enables the two young lovers to come together in an otherwise impossible situation; poised between the "barbarian hordes" and the joyless holy man, is Agnes, an "old beldame," who, though "weak in body and in soul," nevertheless agrees to guide Porphyro to Madeline's chamber. This "aged creature . . . / Shuffling along with ivory-headed wand" appears to be magical in that in her own being she can bridge the gap between two extremes. She recognizes Porphyro and reluctantly agrees to play the part of the deliverer. "Feebly she laugheth in the languid moon, / While Porphyro upon her face doth look, / Like puzzled urchin on an agèd crone." But Agnes helps him nonetheless in preparing a lavish feast, with all manner of delicacies, "of candied apple, quince, and plum, and gourd, / With jellies soother than the creamy curd," and with a table set "cloth of crimson, gold, and jet" and dazzling "golden dishes . . . in baskets bright / Of wreathèd silver."

While watching the chaste Madeline prepare for bed, as she "[u]nclasps her warmed jeweles one by one; / Loosens her fragrant bodice; by degrees" the eroticism of the scene is sanctioned by Porphyro's description of her as "a splendid angel, newly dressed, / Save wings, for Heaven." This procedure of celebrating physical beauty within a sacred context is Keats's version of the biblical "Song of Songs," and it presages the ultimate triumph of physical love. That triumph is possible as Porphyro introduces his own rhetorical version of their escape from the mundane world, telling the sleeping Madeline that their coupling will be their salvation. "And now, my love, my seraph fair, awake! / Thou art my heaven, and I thine eremite." However, that triumph is only possible as the result of both Porphyro's and Madeline's rejection of the contrarieties that enthrall them. While by Madeline's bedside, Porphyro is alarmed by the noisy throng: "The boisterous, midnight, festive clarion, / The kettle-drum and far-heard clarionet, / Affray his ears." Likewise, Madeline must forego her pleasant dreams of romantic opulence and the indulgence of a literary convention that made unrequited love an art.

Thus, Porphyro awakens his lover by the very same seductive thoughts that lulled her to sleep, and in so doing, he uses the same literary convention as a means of consummating his love for Madeline: "and in chords that tenderest be, / He played an ancient ditty, long since mute, / In Provence called, 'La belle dame sans mercy." That spell, "the blisses of her dream so pure and deep," persists even though she is now awake, but it is finally broken as Porphyro becomes a part of that lingering vision. "Into her dream he melted, as the rose / Blendeth its odour with the violet, / Solution sweet."

Having now been joined in the here and now, the story of the two lovers picks up a breathless pace. They must quickly leave lest their love be destroyed by the cold, bleak, and destructive environs of the world they have rejected. "'Tis dark; quick pattereth the flaw-blown sleet," but happily, it is "an elfin-storm from fairy land, / Of haggard seeming, but a boon indeed" that comes to help the lovers make their escape. And so they finally leave a world whose authority is based on the power of illusion and the fear that accompanies it. Madeline "hurried at his words, beset with fears, / For there were sleeping dragons all around, / At glaring watch, perhaps, with ready spears." They disappear into an enchanting storm while the "warrior-guests, with shade and form / . . . / Were long be-nightmared." ❀

Critical Views on
"The Eve of St. Agnes"

GARY FARNELL ON PAGANISM AND THE NATURE OF
FANTASY

[Gary Farnell is the author of "Rereading Shelley" (1993). In
the excerpt below from his article, "'Unfit for Ladies': Keats's
The Eve of St. Agnes," Farnell reads the poem in terms of its
paganism and the transgressive nature of fantasy.]

Keats is a pagan poet. His references are predominantly classical. In
Endymion and the fragment of "Hyperion," the poet's two most
significant works preceding the composition of *The Eve of St. Agnes*,
classical mythology is used as a means of explaining, in a secular
way, the psychological complexity of consuming spiritual states.
Endymion is visited nightly in his sleep by the moon-goddess Diana.
As a result, the dreams he has are equally as beautiful as they are
fleeting. Hereafter, he is destined to discover what is always going to
be to his mind a want of vividness in his waking perceptions. Keats's
poem dramatizes a certain vindication of the dreamer who pursues
his ideal in the face of the disappointing real, even as the pitfalls of
such a pursuit are brought fully into view:

> there are
> Richer entanglements, enthralments far
> More self-destroying, leading, by degrees,
> To the chief intensity.
> ⟨...⟩

Keats's paganism, then, emerges in the extent to which this poet
chooses to identify himself spiritually with the belief-system of
classical mythology, in contrast to that of, say, the contemporary
Christian church. Indeed, although the poet takes an explicit interest
in the specific iconology of the Christian faith in both *The Eve of St.
Agnes* and "The Eve of St. Mark," his concern is in fact to expose
what is seen as the basic iniquity of church values, rules and
practices. The world of *The Eve of St. Agnes*, as embodied in such
figures as the Beadsman, the lords in the hall and even the old nurse
Angela, is essentially prohibitive and life-denying and therefore, as
the actions of Madeline and Porphyro suggest, something to be

defied and escaped from. The world of (the unfinished) "The Eve of St. Mark," as embodied in such figures as the old townsfolk in their "staid and pious companies" and indeed (as legend has it) the Christian martyr of St. Mark himself, is similarly associated more with death than life. Consequently, it comes as little surprise that Bertha should prefer to continue reading her "curious volume. . . [containing] golden broideries" than attend "even song and vesper prayer." Clearly, the transgressive nature of fantasy is being afforded a privilege in both these poems by Keats. So, the poet stands in an ambiguous relation to the details of the popular superstitions which lie behind them: he finds such material useful as a basis for poetic compositions; he is taken by its force even as he refuses to endorse its substance.

On these terms, Keats is clearly interested above all in the issue of what such details, by their popularity, have to say about the sheer forcefulness of fantasy itself. The terms of the St. Agnes ritual—whereby a maid must go supperless to bed without glancing behind her in order to dream of her future husband—are powerful enough to condition even a kind of *Romeo and Juliet*-type of adventure, a negotiating of the antagonisms and tensions of two feuding families, as undertaken romantically by Madeline and Porphyro. Similarly, the terms of the St. Mark ritual—whereby every third year the ghosts of those who will die that particular year can be observed passing before the church porch—are powerful enough to condition even the tragic shortening of the lives of those who, albeit imaginarily, are identified as victims. In this respect, there is doubtless an element of what can be described as the naïve idealist in Keats; the notion that things can be changed just by imagining them differently evidently has some sway in the poet's thought. The "And many pleasures to my vision started" of "I stood tip-toe upon a little hill," for instance, tends to come to mind as a case in point: "what those words *represent*," Marjorie Levinson suggests, pointing to the actual text of this poem, "is their own hermetic interrelatedness. . . . The run-on verbosity of the poem images an author transfixed by his contemplative acts, a prisoner of the fetish-world he engenders." Stylistically, Keats is often found wanting in his poetry, even to the point of pathology.

But beyond this, in the poet's continued commitment to the forcefulness of dreaming and imagining there are available for reclamation, as it were, the traits in his writing of an undeniably sophisticated understanding of the nature of fantasy, of its meaning and of its importance for the structuring of social relations. After all, the narrative of *The Eve of St. Agnes*, for instance, is nothing other than a story of two people's dreams, in a very real and demonstrably practical sense, coming true. Artificially stimulated by Porphyro engaged in turning the terms of the St. Agnes ritual to their mutual advantage, Madeline beholds actually before her eyes upon waking the following morning what is described as "the vision of her sleep." Despite the potential dubiety of its sexual politics, the legend of St. Agnes has indeed been fulfilled. John Jones remarks, endeavoring to take the full stylistic scope of Keats into account, that "*St. Agnes* is the most lavishly confident and affirmative, the happiest of his major poems."

—Gary Farnell, "'Unfit for Ladies': Keats's *The Eve of St. Agnes*," *Studies in Romanticism* 34 no. 3 (Fall 1995): pp. 402–4.

ⓖ

JACQUELINE BANERJEE ON SHAKESPEARE'S ILL-FATED LOVERS AND THE POEM

[Jacqueline Banerjee is the author of *Through the Northern Gate: Childhood and Growing Up in British Fiction, 1719–1901* (1996) and "The Impossible Goal: The Struggle for Manhood in Victorian Fiction" (1996). In the excerpt below from her article, "Mending the Butterfly: The New Historicism and Keats's 'Eve of St. Agnes,'" Banerjee discusses some of the narrative aspects in the poem, contrasting it to Shakespeare's *Romeo and Juliet*, and provides a counter-reading of such phrases "rose-*bloom*" to reveal some of the poem's disturbing elements.]

Several different kinds of historicism are now being advocated and practiced by literary critics on both sides of the Atlantic. Common to all of them is the view of literature as the site of an ideological struggle; but some prominent American critics are prepared to show how the written work transcends this struggle, while other more radical critics are only interested in finding material in the work to support their own political stances. Those who practice a more broadly humanist and less strident vein of the New Historicism seem to me the most illuminating. ⟨...⟩

Indeed, definitions themselves are invidious, because by their very nature they exclude and privilege, both of which activities are anathema to contemporary critical practice. Still, in general it might safely be said that the New Historicists, like the Cultural Materialists, consider a literary work more as a cultural than a linguistic construct. ⟨...⟩

"The Eve of St. Agnes" is a peculiarly apt work to discuss in this context. For one thing, it has traditionally been read as a poem built on the conflict between the romantic dream and the grim circumstances which surround it; for another, this time-honored interpretation has itself proved vulnerable to attack by a new generation of ideologically motivated critics.

On the narrative level, Keats has produced a version of the Romeo and Juliet story, as an impetuous young man named Porphyro braves a hostile household to elope with his adored and adoring Madeline. The young lovers' passion and fool-hardy courage is thrown into relief not only by reference to the bloodthirsty inmates of the stronghold from which Porphyro abducts his sweetheart, but also by descriptions of two old people: the ancient Beadsman, whose job it is to pray for ancestral souls in the family chapel, and Angela, a motherly old crone who aids and abets Porphyro, taking a similar role to that of Juliet's nurse in Shakespeare's play or a fairy godmother in fairy tales. While the lovers escape into love's young dream, apparently demonstrating their own "power and transcendence," these two old folk are consigned to death at the end. However, all this takes place in the long ago and far away, since Keats chooses a rich setting of medieval romance. Moreover, it takes place on St. Agnes's Eve, an evening in late January when a girl who obeys certain rituals may be favored by the saint with a vision of her lover. Love's young dream *is* only a dream, after all, and, to borrow McGann's phraseology again, "the facts of [its] limits" are very clear. The storm into which the couple flee must eventually envelop them just as the realities of age and death envelop the Beadsman and Angela. It is known that one of the inspirations for the poem was an Italian fresco "The Triumph of Death," which Keats's painter friend Haydon had recently shown him prints of. In other words, the conflict in the narrative is paralleled by a conflict in the theme. It would seem that although the focus is on Porphyro and Madeline, the reality of the poem is located elsewhere. In this way, the poem can be seen as a moving allegory of the human condition, with Keats himself yearning over the splendor of romance but poignantly recognizing its limitations. This reading does of course posit a manipulating author, not one who is in fact being manipulated by the ideals and ideologies of his age.

However, like the romantic dream it clings to, the orthodox exposition of "The Eve of St. Agnes" proves fragile on closer inspection. From the very first stanza, Formalist attention to the choice, positioning and sounds of words raises questions about its validity:

> St. Agnes' Eve—Ah, bitter chill it was!
> The owl, for all his feathers, was a-cold;
> The hare limp'd trembling through the frozen grass,
> And silent was the flock in woolly fold:
> Numb were the Beadsman's fingers, while he told
> His rosary, and while his frosted breath,
> Like pious incense from a censer old,
> Seem'd taking flight for heaven, without a death,
> Past the sweet Virgin's picture, while his prayer he saith.

Words signifying coldness, silence, and death-like feebleness or pallor are foregrounded in this stanza by a sequence of three grammatical inversions—"*chill* it was"; "*silent* was the flock"; and "*numb* were the Beadsman's fingers," with a particularly empathic one in the very first line, which is also an exclamation. Not only the semantic and syntactic correspondences but the sequence itself is significant. The resistance to activity or expression—even before the verb arrives, the action is restricted—builds up until, with the word "numb," even feeling stops. ⟨. . .⟩

Another famous stanza, which radiates love, color, and warmth, also has a puzzling undertow. This is stanza 25, in which moonlight, colored as it passes through a gorgeous stained-glass window, glorifies Madeline as she prays in her bedroom:

> Full on this casement shone the wintry moon,
> And threw warm gules on Madeline's fair breast,
> As down she knelt for heaven's grace and boon;
> Rose-bloom fell on her hands together prest,
> And on her silver cross soft amethyst,

And on her hair a glory, like a saint:
She seem'd a splendid angel, newly drest,
Save wings, for heaven:—Porphyro grew faint:
She knelt, so pure a thing, so free from mortal taint.

Madeline's glowing appearance here is beloved of critics who find this work quite simply "one of the most delightful poems in the English language." The associations of the moon with feminine beauty and chastity, and the added connotations of maturity and ripeness for love in the rich compound word "rose-*bloom*," enhances such critics' delight. As for the word "gules," denoting red in the language of heraldry, at first sight this contributes to the sense impressions already received, with the added advantage of connecting Madeline with her noble ancestral past. Also noted by generations of critics is the way that the young woman's richly physical presence is shot through with suggestions of otherworldliness, culminating in the word "heaven" in the last line of the stanza. ⟨. . .⟩

Again, however, verbal correspondences and patterns of syntax and vowel sounds reveal some disturbing elements. The moonlight "throws" the "gules" on Madeline's "fair breast," reminding us of the "hot-blooded lords" in Madeline's aristocratic family who would not hesitate to spill Porphyro's blood and (no doubt) break Madeline's heart. Madeline is not only intensely vulnerable but also utterly passive as the light falls first "on" the window and then "on" various parts of her (the preposition is repeated five times). ⟨. . .⟩

> —Jacqueline Banerjee, "Mending the Butterfly: The New Historicism and Keats's 'Eve of St. Agnes,'" *College English* 57, no. 5 (September 1995): pp. 529–31, 533–35.

⊗

ANDREW J. BENNETT ON SEEING AND UNSEEING

[Andrew J. Bennett is the author of *Keats, Narrative, and Audience: The Posthumous Life of Writing* (1994) and *Romantic Poets and the Culture of Posterity* (1999). In the excerpt below from his article, "'Hazardous Magic': Vision and Inscription in Keats's 'The Eve of St. Agnes,'" Bennett

[discusses the significance of various tensions within the poem, such as the opposition between waking and sleeping as well as the interruption of the narrative process.]

As a number of critics have noted, "The Eve of St. Agnes" involves a double plot, or, at least, a double plotting: while Porphyro requires a visual embodiment of his desires and a physical consummation of those desires, Madeline requires a vision of her desires and a visionary dream of a consummation. This provides Keats with the narrative friction/irritation that generates the poem. But around this friction of plotting may be discerned several other frictions: the friction of gender—male/female desires; the friction of narration—the production and disruption of narrative in description; the friction of the antagonism of the visionary to the visible; the friction of sleep/waking; the friction of response—the conflict between the desires of the poet and those of his reader; and the (related) friction of the reader's gender—the question of male/female reception. Friction generates heat, just as irritability generates life in the eighteenth- and nineteenth-century discourse of physiology: out of the frictions and irritations of "St. Agnes" Keats produced his most seductive narrative poem. And perhaps the most decisive and influential binary opposition in the twentieth-century criticism of "The Eve of St. Agnes," that between the transcendentalism of Wasserman and the voyeurism of Stillinger, may be understood in terms of description, which, as Michel Beaujour has pointed out, constitutes the contradictory locus of the utopian and the voyeuristic.

The central narrative impulsion that draws together the frictions of Keats's fiction is Porphyro's desire for the vision of Madeline (her sight and the sight of her; Porphyro's visual vision of Madeline and her visionary vision of him; his seeing and her un-seeing eyes; he unseen and she seen). Not only does the description of Porphyro watching Madeline undress in stanzas 24–26 provide one of the narrative cruxes of the poem (the others being the physical consummation of this visible vision at stanza 36—a consummation in itself sublimated into the language of sight—and the displaced consummation of the inedible, the visual feast in stanza 30), but it also provides the most explicit—the most visible—locus of chiastic interaction with the reader. It is at this point of seeing, more than at any other point in the poem, that the questions of the gender of the reader, his/her (dis)taste, ethical judgment, vision, and desire are most clearly posed: Madeline's undressing impels questions such as what a female reader is to make of Porphyro's pleasure, whether the poem should be read as a vulgar adolescent fantasy of voyeurism, the intentions (honorable or otherwise) of Porphyro, the extent to which readers (male here, presumably) are implicated in an unreflexive ocular violence towards Madeline, the extent to which the poet can make the reader "see," and the question of the congruence of Porphyro's desire with that of the (again male?) reader. Moreover, the fact that narration is generated by desire in Prophyro, the narrator, and ultimately the reader for this antinarratorial (or descriptive) epiphany of watching Madeline means that the mechanics of narrative form may be most clearly interrogated at this climactic moment. The fact that the poetry constantly refers to, entices, and describes visual perception, suggests that the internal duality of the visionary/visible is doubled in the relationship of the reader with the poem.

In "The Eve of St. Agnes" the narrative is impelled by vision: looking organizes both the plot and the reader's relationship with the action. At the same time looking produces a resistance to narration as the characters and narrator attempt to fix the look and halt the narrative. It is, above all, the narrative friction of the double plot in "The Eve of St. Agnes"—Madeline's plot to "see" her lover and Porphyro's plot to see his—that produces the narrative friction generative of the complex of narrative relationships—narrator to reader, narrator to narrative, reader to text. ⟨. . .⟩

While Porphyro is intent on seeing, Madeline is continually presented as unseeing. Part of this blindness is a requirement of tradition, the convention that in order to have a "vision of delight" virgins must "Nor look behind, nor sideways, but require / Of heaven with upward eyes for all that they desire." The upward eyes are not looking at all—they "require" rather than look—for heaven is to be apprehended through vision and not through eyesight. Another aspect of Madeline's blindness is her refusal to see what she does not want to: as she waits to leave the party she "heed[s] not at all" the other guests and refuses to see the "armorous cavalier[s]." Similarly, her "regardless eyes" refuse to see because it is a visionary vision she requires, and Keats makes no bones about her blindness to "reality": she is "Hoodwink'd with faery fancy." What Madeline "sees" are "visions wide" or waking dreams: "Pensive awhile she dreams awake, and sees, / In fancy, fair St. Agnes in her bed, / But dares not look behind, or all the charm is fled." ⟨...⟩

—Andrew J. Bennett, "'Hazardous Magic': Vision and Inscription in Keats's 'The Eve of St. Agnes,'" *Keats-Shelley Journal* 41 (1992): pp. 101–3.

⟨๑⟩

JOHN COLLICK ON DESIRE IN THE POEM

[John Collick is the author of *Shakespeare, Cinema and Society* (1989). In the excerpt below from his article, "Desire on 'The Eve of St. Agnes,'" Collick discusses the element of desire within the poem and its relationship to such other literary works as the gothic novel and *Romeo and Juliet*.]

John Keats has generally been thought of as one of the least 'worldly' of the Romantic poets. Harold Bloom summed up this approach by stating that 'Keats is grimly free of tradition in his subtle implication of a truth that most of us learn. Poetry is not a means of good; it is ... like the honey of earth that comes and goes at once, while we wait vainly for the honey of heaven'. In other words Keats's poems continually attempt to recreate transient moments of fleeting beauty and alternate between intense, physical images and complaints that such moments can never endure. The impression is that Keats, unlike the more down-to-earth Wordsworth, Coleridge or Shelley, was entirely given over to the image of the Romantic poet as the tragic figure hovering between this world and the next. ⟨...⟩

Another reading of Keats's poems can be made, one in which language itself is acknowledged as political. Recent literary theory has focused on the relationship between language and ideology. To give a broad definition: ideology is a system of beliefs that conceals the power relationships within society. Its basic medium is language, the structures of which offer individuals a certain perception of the world as natural and given. Critics have suggested that each individual is constructed through language. In other words our perception of ourselves (the 'I') is a location within a linguistic framework of meaning which we occupy after we are born. However, ideology has its gaps where language becomes inadequate. One such area is desire. Society in Keats's day imposed very rigid sexual roles on people. The control of desire, particularly in women, was a fundamental means of securing social, family-based stability. Because sexuality was imposed through language, desire itself was silent; it could not speak for itself. Was Keats aware of the political nature of language and did he set out to use his poetry to highlight its inability to express desire? ⟨...⟩

Thus there is a strange ambiguity in Keats's work. For a poet concerned with dreams, visions and images trembling on the point of dissolution, such concrete, sensual imagery seems out of place, it destroys the transcendent atmosphere of the passage in which it is set. Keats's deflationary passages don't merely consist of such direct references. He also uses a wide range of euphemisms, some of which appear to be displaced representations of sex and sexual desire. In his poetry I believe that Keats was investigating the process by which hidden, forbidden and impossible desires are transferred onto symbolic objects. This would explain the passage in 'The Eve of St. Agnes' when Angela the maid tells Porphyro that, by hiding in Madeline's closet, he will be able to see his lady's 'own lute'. Later on I will look at displaced representations of sexual desire in more detail. ⟨...⟩

On the surface 'The Eve of St. Agnes' seems to have all the trappings of a Keats poem about the destruction of the visionary by grubby reality; set in a Gothic world. Yet this description is deceptive because it fails to take into account two important elements in the poem. Firstly the poem can be read as a parody of the Gothic genre and, secondly, Keats fills it with a very self-conscious mixture of symbols representing poems and symbols representing sex. If read from this point of view 'The Eve of St. Agnes' ceases to be a Gothic drama that borrows heavily from *Romeo and Juliet*. It virtually becomes a protracted satire at the expense of those writers who tried to use both the Gothic and poetry itself to express sexual desire.

The Gothic novel was a genre that reached its peak at the end of the eighteenth century. It was immensely popular, especially among women readers. Most Gothic tales were set in a quasi-medieval past and featured crumbling fortresses, villains, ghosts and bandits. A female readership rigidly constrained by the morality of eighteenth-century society readily identified with heroines who were victimised by sneering oppressors, imprisoned in nunneries and terrified by spectres. A continual theme that ran through the Gothic, and spilled over into other genres, was the impossibility of fulfilling desire. ⟨. . .⟩

In broader terms the theme of dynastic oppression is symbolised both by the barbaric revels of the castle's inhabitants and the imagery of cold statues, shields and ancient legends. The heroine, Madeline, is especially singled out as a victim of this. 'Asleep in the lap of legends old' her existence is determined by her position within a society that uses women as commodities to be bargained for and exchanged. The fact that Keats describes Madeline as sleeping in the lap of a *legend* seems to suggest that her oppression is partly linguistic. In a sense the poem itself is a legend in which Madeline sleeps in symbolic terms. This is compounded by the fact that Porphyro learns this from Old Angela who is like 'an aged crone / Who keepeth clos'd a wond'rous riddle-book'.

Old legends and the wondrous riddle book are not the only references to the construction of poetry within 'The Eve of St. Agnes'. The work is full of images of tapestries, illuminated windows and still-life groups that can all be seen as displaced metaphors for the poem itself. Furthermore these symbols are used to explore the impossibility of expressing desire through poetic language. The most illuminating example of this can be seen in verses 23 and 24. Porphyro, having hidden in the closet of Madeline's chamber, watches as she enters the room. Madeline, forbidden to speak by the enchantment, suffers the agony of someone filled by an inspiration she is unable to give vent to:

> She clos'd the door, she panted, all akin
> To spirits of the air, and visions wide:
> No uttered syllable, or, woe betide!
> But to her heart, her heart was voluble,
> Paining with eloquence her balmy side;
> As though a tongueless nightingale should swell
> Her throat in vain, and die, heart stifled, in her dell. ⟨. . .⟩

—John Collick, "Desire on 'The Eve of St. Agnes,'" *Critical Survey* 3, no. 1 (1991): pp. 37–39.

KAREN J. HARVEY ON MERLIN AND THE LADY OF THE LAKE

[In the excerpt below from her article, "The Trouble about Merlin: The Theme of Enchantment in 'The Eve of St. Agnes,'" Karen J. Harvey focuses on the figure of Merlin in the Arthurian legend, and suggests that the true "incubus" in Keats's poem may in fact be Merlin's lover, the Lady of the Lake.]

Enchantment is a major theme in the medieval realm of "The Eve of St. Agnes," in which Keats portrays a world of sorcery, charm, and spell. Throughout the poem the reader is presented with persistent imagery of "faery fancy" and magic. The young knight Porphyro is aided in his quest for the love of the maiden Madeline by an aged beldame who carries an "ivory-headed wand" and is seen by him as an old crone "who keepeth clos'd a wond'rous riddle-book." Madeline, the object of Porphyro's pursuit on the eve of St. Agnes, plays "the conjuror." "Legion'd fairies" pace the coverlet in her bedchamber, where "pale enchantment" holds her as "St. Agnes' charmed maid." When she enters her bedroom where Porphyro is hiding, she is "all akin / To spirits of the air." Once she sleeps, he despairs of bringing her out of "such a stedfast spell"; when she awakens, he fears to move or speak because of her strange dreaming look. Indeed, "'twas a midnight charm / Impossible to melt." As St. Agnes' moon sets, a storm arises, described by Porphyro as "an elfin-storm from faery land," into which the lovers flee. They leave behind the baron and the revelers, whose dreams are occupied by "shade and form / Of witch and demon."

In perhaps the most striking passage reflecting this theme of magic and enchantment, Keats writes of the eve that "Never on such a night have lovers met, / Since Merlin paid his Demon all the monstrous debt." Attempts to determine the meaning of these lines and their relationship to the poem have presented readers with problems of interpretation that M. R. Ridley has characterized aptly as "the trouble about Merlin." There is general agreement that the two lines obviously allude to Arthurian legend; beyond this, critical commentary on the passage has often been marked by diversity and contradiction. ⟨...⟩

As stated earlier, the "demon" in the Merlin allusion has often been understood as the incubus who fathered the future wizard. However, an examination of, first, the nature and characteristics of a fay and, second, Keats's use of the term in his poetry, may provide another possibility—Vivien. For the Celtic *fay*, or in its British form *fairy*, is not the beneficent figure of children's fairy-tales, whose antisocial behavior tends to be at most mischievous. The Celtic, and later Arthurian, fay or fairy-woman is a powerful enchantress, who can be kind and solicitous to those whom she favors, but also malign and cruel to those who displease her. The fairies of British folklore also have their darker side. Contacts with fays and fairies, particularly with the female figure of the fairy-mistress, are often sinister and ominous, indeed dangerous. This is a reflection not only of the general association of fairies with spirits of the dead, but, even more important, of the fairy-mistress's well-known predilection, attested in both Celtic and British folklore, for detaining or imprisoning her lover.

Folkloric descriptions of fairy activities provide numerous examples of association with those linked to demons—the raising of storms, the abduction of children, and the spoiling of crops. Lines of division between the two are frequently blurred, and the world of Faery is often shadowed by that of the demonic. ⟨. . .⟩

Moreover, an examination of Keats's use of the word "demon" in his poetry reveals a striking pattern. When it is used in a thematic sense and applied to a specific character, "demon" invariably refers to a female who bewitches and enthralls her male adorer, with fateful consequences for him. ⟨. . .⟩ In "Lamia" the "demon" is the serpent who, transformed into a woman by the god Hermes, enthralls the young Corinthian Lycius. Lamia, who "seem'd, at once, some penanced lady elf, / Some demon's mistress, or the demon's self," has the familiar effect of the enchantress on her male adorer: Lycius "Swoon'd, murmuring of love, and pale with pain," and becomes "tangled in her mesh." Their love ends when her real nature is discovered by Apollonius the philosopher: Lamia vanishes and Lycius dies. Both the fairy tradition's association with the demonic and Keats's use of "demon" suggest, then, that "his Demon" in the Merlin allusion could refer not just to the incubus, but to Vivien as well—in terms of both her nature as fay and her effect on Merlin, the male who adores her and has been enthralled by her to disastrous effect.

As for the phrase "Never on such a night," it may well, as one commentator has suggested, refer exclusively to the meeting of Madeline and Porphyro on the eve of St. Agnes, "a night of magic and enchantment such as has not been seen since Merlin's magical powers left the world." There is, however, a version of Merlin's fate that may make a reference to nighttime pertinent in terms of the Arthurian tale. A thirteenth-century continuation of the Merlin legend known as the *Suite de Merlin* tells of Merlin and Vivien's journey to the forest of Broceliande in Brittany. He shows her where two lovers are buried in a great rock, and she, taken with the lovers' tale, wishes to spend the night in their tomb. When Merlin falls asleep, Vivien, using the magical powers she has learned from him, imprisons him there. This version refers specifically to "la nuit elle enchante Merlin" and was used by Malory in *Morte D' Arthur*, which is the basis for most subsequent English treatments of the Merlin tale.

—Karen J. Harvey, "The Trouble about Merlin: The Theme of Enchantment in 'The Eve of St. Agnes,'" *Keats-Shelley Journal* 34 (1985): pp. 83–88.

Thematic Analysis of
"Ode to a Nightingale"

According to a letter written by Keats's friend, Charles Brown, Keats's inspiration for the "Ode to a Nightingale" occurred while he sat under a plum tree one spring morning, listening for two or three hours to the tranquil and continuously joyful song of a nightingale. Upon reentering Brown's house, Keats held several scraps of paper on which he had written about his poetic feelings. Brown later discovered them hidden behind some books. The poem was written in a single morning, probably in early April or May 1819, both preceding and inspiring Keats's other great odes, including the "Ode on a Grecian Urn."

As in all of the odes considered within this study, a theme that runs consistently throughout the lines is that of the human wish to transcend the ravages of time and decay and the poetic struggle to create an original and enduring work that surpasses all others. As will be seen, the wish for permanence, both for the artist and the work of art, is a recurring one for Keats.

In the **first stanza**, the speaker addresses the object of his desire, the nightingale of "melodious" song that "singest of summer in full-throated ease." The poet protests that he is not envious of the bird's "happy lot." Rather, he professes disinterested concern for the nightingale that has no knowledge of its own mortality, "being too happy in thine happiness." However, though the speaker claims that his concern is for the nightingale's innocent joy, as we will see, the speaker actually wants to identify with the bird—to compose melodious verse, for which the genre of the ode is especially appropriate and, most important, to remove himself from the sorrows of mortal experience by becoming one with the nightingale. The achievement of this desire will require a complex series of radical, rhetorical gestures.

That process begins in the first lines of the "Ode to a Nightingale" as the speaker attempts to erase what he already knows about the ravages of time through a self-imposed forgetfulness. However, these gestures are fraught with tension, and thus they threaten to invalidate the speaker's efforts, forcing him to return to the mundane world of human sensibility he so desperately seeks to leave behind, "where men sit and hear each other groan." "A drowsy numbness pains / My sense, as though of hemlock I had drunk, / . . . One minute past, and Lethe-wards had sunk." The speaker is so despondent that he is willing to take hemlock, a poisonous herb, so as to forget his former life, and even descend to the mythic underworld of Hades to drink of the waters of Lethe, the river of forgetfulness.

In the **second stanza**, having left his cares behind, the speaker now prays for inspiration from sources that reside in both ancient and medieval systems of belief. He wishes to taste the wine ("a draught of vintage!") produced by Flora, the ancient Roman goddess of flowering plants, thus again pointing to the wish to blossom as a poet. In the speaker's enthusiasm to become as mellifluous as the nightingale, he is reminded of the troubadours of medieval Provence, lyric poets from southern France who sang of courtly love.

The concept of courtly love, however, is but an elaborate literary convention, dealing with such themes as humility and devotion to a lady, a farewell to earthly existence upon an imminent departure for a crusade, and the deferred or impossible consummation of love with the lady of whom one sings. The troubadours were also responsible for writing both text and melody for their poems, and these were often performed by a *jogleur* (a singing messenger). Both troubadours and jogleurs traveled widely, and as a result, they contributed to the diffusion of the art form into other languages.

Thus, Keats's reference to Provençal song is a composite of many of his own poetic aspirations. At the close of stanza two and into the beginning of the third stanza, we are once again reminded of his desire to be united with the nightingale and thereby transcend the mundane world to which he feels fettered. "That I might drink, and leave the world unseen, / And with thee fade away into the forest dim: Fade far away, dissolve, and quite forget / What thou amongst the leaves hast never known." The commonplace world is one in which the poet can only hear jarring and fretful sounds and observe the ravages of time. "Where palsy shakes a few, sad, last gray hairs, / Where youth grows pale / . . . Where but to think is to be full of sorrow." As we saw in the first stanza, the effort Keats must expend in leaving the world behind is a strenuous act of imagination and continually overshadowed with uncertainty, for he cannot become one with the nightingale.

In contrast to the literary inspiration that he summons in the second stanza, in the **third stanza** we find him rejecting those same muses, "[n]ot charioted by Bacchus and his pards." This denial is significant, because Bacchus, also called Dionysus, was the most versatile and elusive of the Greek gods, associated first and foremost with wine and intoxication. Perceived as both human and divine, male and female, young and old, Bacchus is also associated with the ability to transcend the boundaries of human experience. Here in the fourth stanza, the speaker rejects the unbridled passions of an ecstatic ancient muse, preferring an invisible and far less self-conscious source of inspiration, expressed in the wish to ascend on "the viewless wings of Poesy." Though "the dull brain perplexes and retards," both slowing the flight of imagination and rendering its thoughts difficult to grasp, the speaker prefers the delicate sensibilities of the nightingale and its consoling song. "Already with thee! Tender is the night."

Keats's banishment of intense emotion from the creative process and his embracing of a far more tempered and contemplative mode of production is problematic, however, for he must now wend his way through a dark and uncharted path, a darkness that can be only partially alleviated. "But here there is no light, / Save what from heaven is . . . / Through verdurous glooms and winding mossy ways."

This crisis intensifies in the **fifth stanza**. "I cannot see what flowers are at my feet, / Nor what soft incense hangs upon the boughs, / But, in embalmed darkness, guess each sweet." Apparently, the exchange of Bacchus's divine ecstasy and heightened awareness for the muted and rarefied atmosphere of the nightingale has precipitated intense fears and anxieties. The poet has lost the ability to distinguish between nature's bounty and the poet's identification with nature. The natural world is now shielded from the poet's view, leaving him worried about an enterprise that seems to have gone out of control despite his best efforts to contain it. He no longer knows the correct season. Neither can he distinguish the grass from the "white hawthorn" or "the pastoral eglantine," though these same flowers belong to a very long and ancient literary tradition. Rather, the "[f]ast fading violets [are] cover'd up in leaves."

The speaker's dilemma can only intensify in a realm where the functioning of the senses is confused. He declares, "Darkling I listen; and, for many a time / I have been half in love with easeful Death," and he alludes to the "wakeful bird" in Milton's *Paradise Lost*, the formidable voice of the poetic forebear with whom he struggles. The struggle to imaginatively identify with the nightingale now mandates a symbolic death that would liberate the poet from all mortal fears, most especially the anxiety about his own creative abilities. Meanwhile, the nightingale, sensitive to his emotions, now sings a sorrowful song: "Now more than ever seems it rich to die, / To cease upon the midnight with no pain, / While thou art pouring forth thy soul abroad / . . . To thy high requiem become a sod."

The **seventh stanza** begins with an abrupt shift, focusing now both on the poet's desire to be like the nightingale and his implicit acknowledgment that this identification is impossible. The speaker is forced to concede that he must live in the world of mortal cares and transient beauty. "Thou was not born for death, immortal Bird! No hungry generations tread thee down." Thus, his desired fusion with his beloved nightingale can no longer even be imagined, for the bird belongs to a far more distant poetic realm.

That world is found in the poetry of the biblical story of Ruth, who chose to remain with her mother-in-law in a foreign land following the death of her husband: "Perhaps the self-same song that found a path / Through the sad heart of Ruth." Likewise, the nightingale's world is located in the medieval romantic tradition where humans were endowed with supernatural powers and lived in an enchanted, and often perilous, landscape. "The same that oft-times hath / Charm'd magic casements, opening on the foam / Of perilous seas, in faery lands forlorn."

In the **eighth** and **final stanza** the poet uses the word "forlorn" to describe his own feelings of abandonment and desertion. He recognizes now that he and the nightingale are worlds apart and the "viewless wings of Poesy" cannot transport him to a happier place and time. He has lost all hope, and his repetition of the word "forlorn" at the end of the seventh and the beginning of the eighth stanzas is significant; in its older, Middle English form, *forloren*, meant to lose something, which here refers to something intangible, namely the loss of even a promise of future fulfillment. Instead, the bells summon the poet to the reality of his very human nature, and in that return, his cognitive efforts to become one with the nightingale must be left behind. That summoning is accompanied by the sounds of lamentation: "Adieu! The fancy cannot cheat so well / As she is fam'd to do, deceiving elf. / Adieu! Adieu! Thy plaintive anthem fades."

And so the poem ends with the speaker wondering about the very nature of his vision. The wish to transcend the boundaries of mortal existence cannot be granted. "Fled is that music:—Do I wake or sleep?" ❀

Critical Views on
"Ode to a Nightingale"

HAROLD BLOOM ON EMERGING ATTITUDES TOWARD DEATH

[Harold Bloom, the editor of this series, has written extensively on all of the Romantic poets. His books include *The Ringers in the Tower: Studies in the Romantic Tradition* (1971), *The Anxiety of Influence: The Theory of Poetry* (1975) and *Ruin the Sacred Truths: Poetry and Belief from the Bible to the Present* (1989). In the excerpt below, Bloom discusses the sensuous nature of Keats's visionary flight in "Ode to a Nightingale" and the emerging attitude toward death both as an inspiring muse and as a desired state superior to the mortality of the human condition.]

The *Ode to a Nightingale* opens with the hammer beats of three heavily accented syllables—"My heart aches"—signaling the sudden advent of a state of consciousness unlike the Beulah state of "indolence," soft, relaxed, and feminine, which marks Keats's usual mode of heightened awareness and creativity. Like Shelley in the *Skylark,* Keats is listening to an unseen bird whose location he cannot specify—it is "In *some* melodious plot / Of beechen green, and shadows numberless." But the sharp immediacy of its song is nevertheless emphasized, for it sings "of summer in full-throated ease." The effect of the song on Keats is dual and strongly physical, indeed almost deathly. His heart aches, and his sense is pained with a drowsy numbness that suggests, first, having been poisoned; next, having taken a narcotic. Not the sound alone of the song, but Keats's empathizing with the bird, has done this. He is not envious of the bird, but is "too happy" in its happiness. He cannot sustain his own "negative capability" in this case; he has yielded his being too readily to that of the bird.

And yet, he welcomes this dangerous vertigo, for the next stanza of the poem seeks to prolong his condition by its wish for drunkenness, for "a beaker full of the warm South." The slackening intensity from poison to narcotic to wine is itself a return to an ordinary wakeful consciousness, a sense of the usual reality from which Keats here would "fade away into the forest dim," to join the nightingale in its invisibility and enclosed joy; to leave behind the world of mutability, where every increase in consciousness is an increase in sorrow. But the leave-taking is the contrary of Keats's expectation; the flight is not an evasion, but an elaboration of waking reality:

> Away! away! For I will fly to thee,
> > Not charioted by Bacchus and his pards,
> But on the viewless wings of Poesy,
> > Though the dull brain perplexes and retards:
> Already with thee!

Suddenly, having put aside the last aid to invocation, but by the act of writing his poem, he is where he wills to be, with the nightingale. The wings of Poesy are "viewless," not just because they are invisible, but because the flight is too high for a vision of the earth to be possible. And the state that now commences is a puzzle to the retarding "dull brain." The sweep of the imagination here is more than rational in its energy. Between the ecstatic cry of "Already with thee!" and the bell-like tolling of the word "forlorn" at the poem's climax, Keats enters the inner world of his poem, that highest state of the imagination which Blake called Eden. The mystery of Keats's unresolved contraries is in his quite anti-Blakean association of this state of more abundant life with what seems to be the death impulse. What for Blake is a state of greater *vision* is for Keats the realm of the *viewless*:

> Already with thee! tender is the night,
> > And haply the Queen-Moon is on her throne,
> > Cluster'd around by all her starry Fays;
> > > But here there is no light,
> Save what from heaven is with the breezes blown
> Through verdurous glooms and winding mossy ways.

It is the night that is tender, the paradoxical darkness of the Keatsian vision constituting the mark of that tenderness. Nature is not blacked out; moon and stars may be present, but their light must first submit to the diminishing maze through which the night winds are blown.

Sight goes; the other senses abide in this trance, which at once equals nature and poetry. He cannot see, but odor, taste, and sound, in an instructive ordering, are called upon to describe the phenomena of the world he has at once entered and created. First, odor and taste, in the form of "soft incense" and "dewy wine":

> I cannot see what flowers are at my feet,
>> Nor what soft incense hangs upon the boughs,
> But, in embalmed darkness, guess each sweet
>> Wherewith the seasonable month endows
> The grass, the thicket, and the fruit-tree wild;
>> White hawthorn, and the pastoral eglantine:
>> Fast fading violets cover'd up in leaves;
>> And mid-May's eldest child,
> The coming musk-rose, full of dewy wine,
> The murmurous haunt of flies on summer eves.

The sensuous imagery here is the luxury of the lower paradise, of the Gardens of Adonis or of Beulah, but set in a context more severe. The odors and tastes are almost those of a more abandoned Milton, a blind poet intensifying the glory he cannot apprehend. But this is closer to the blindness of faith, the evidence of things not seen. Keats cannot see the flowers, but they do him homage at his feet. The "soft incense hangs upon the boughs" for him; and the darkness is "embalmed," a hint of the death wish in the next stanza. The month has kept faith; it is seasonable, and so aids Keats in guessing the identity of each odor. ⟨. . .⟩

Two attitudes toward death, the first shading into the second, are involved in this beautiful but disturbed stanza. Previous to the occasion this ode celebrates, the poet says, he has frequently invoked Death, under his "soft names" of ease, calling on Death to take his breathing spirit "into the air," that is, to die by the very act of exhaling. As he has called upon Death in "many a mused rhyme," this exhaling is equivalent to the act of uttering and composing his poem, and we are reminded that spirit means both soul and breath, and that the poet invoking his muse calls upon a breath greater than his own to inspirit him. Death, then, is here a muse, but this was previously only partly the case:

> I have been *half* in love with easeful Death.

But

> Now more than ever seems it rich to die,
>> To cease upon the midnight with no pain.

"Rich" and "cease" are marvelously precise words. Now, in the shared communion of the darkness out of which the nightingale's song emerges, it seems rich to die, and he is *more than half* in love with easeful Death. For he has reached the height of living experience, and any descent out of this state into the poverty of ordinary consciousness seems a death-in-life, a pain to be avoided, in contrast to the life-in-death "with no pain" to be maintained were he "to cease upon the midnight." "To cease," suddenly not to be, and thus to cross over into non-being attended by the "requiem," the high mass of the nightingale's song. For the nightingale itself is pouring forth its soul abroad in an ecstasy that transcends the division between life and death; the bird lives, but its breath-soul is taken into the air as it gives itself freely in the extension of its ecstasy.

—Harold Bloom, *The Visionary Company: A Reading of English Romantic Poetry* (Ithaca: Cornell University Press, 1961): pp. 407–11.

⊗

EARL R. WASSERMAN ON THE RELATIONSHIP BETWEEN POET AND NIGHTINGALE

[Earl R. Wasserman is the author of *Aspects of the Eighteenth Century* (1965), *The Finer Tone: Keats' Major Poems* (1967), and *Shelley: A Critical Reading* (1971). In the excerpt below, Wasserman discusses the problem of contentment and balance in the human condition in the "Ode to a Nightingale," and reveals various levels of abstraction in the relationship between the poet and the nightingale.]

The conflict out of which the ode is born is a recurrent one in Keats' poetry and is the inevitable result of the oxymoronic ontology within which he thinks. The poet's self has been caught up in empathic ecstasy so completely that he is "too happy." The absorption into essence—the fellowship divine which constitutes "happiness"—has been greater than is destined for mortal man, and the result is heartache and painful numbness. The ideal condition towards which Keats always strives because it is his ideal, is one in which mortal and immortal, dynamism and stasis, the Dionysian and the Apollonian, beauty and truth, are one. And in the "Ode on a Grecian Urn" and "La Belle Dame Sans Merci" he had traced mortal man's momentary ascent to, and his inevitable eviction from, this condition. But if, in his aspirations towards the conditions of heaven's bourne, man is unable to draw heaven and earth together into a stable union—and it is part of Keats' scheme of things that he must be unable while he is mortal—then he is torn between the two extremes, grasping after both but at home in neither. ⟨. . .⟩ If man could confine his aspirations to this physical world, to "something of material sublime," he might find a degree of content; but it is of his very nature that, unless he limits himself to the "level chambers" of mere revelry, he can no more renounce his quest for the ideal than Endymion can renounce his quest for Cynthia. ⟨. . .⟩

It is precisely in this maddening "Purgatory blind" that is neither earth nor heaven, and from which both seem without their pleasant hues, that the "Ode to a Nightingale" has its being. It is a poem without any standard law to which to refer, oscillating between heaven and earth and never able to reconcile them. The ode begins after the point that had been attained in the third stanza of the "Ode on a Grecian Urn." That poem, by enacting the ascent to a condition of happiness, could then salvage from the shattered momentary experience the meaning that the extra-human ascent has in the context of human existence; the "Ode to a Nightingale," however, by beginning with the dissolution itself, can only trace its further disintegration. It is necessary to recognize clearly this initial condition of the poet, for the significance of the entire poem is dependent upon it. Because the poem begins after the height of the empathic experience and traces the further journey homeward to habitual self, we are to look for irreconcilables, not harmonies; for patterns flying apart, not coming together; for conflicting standards.

Briefly, we are to read it by an inversion of the perspectives that give the "Ode on a Grecian Urn" its meaning. Or, better, we are to recognize the irony whereby Keats translates the experience with the nightingale into the terms of one who is being drawn back to the mortal world, and not one who, as in the other ode, is progressing towards the bourne of heaven. The thematic materials of the two odes, we shall see, are the same; but what blends organically in the "Ode on a Grecian Urn" disintegrates in this ode; what is seen in its immortal aspects in the former is seen in its mortal aspects in the latter. ⟨. . .⟩

But let us now invert this movement. As we retreat from passionate selflessness, the two elements separate out of their organic union into strong emotion and a loss of self. And if then we evaluate these two, not as they carry us towards the dynamic stasis of heaven, but as they appear within the framework of merely mortal experience, the powerful emotion becomes only painfully exquisite sensation, and the selflessness only a swooning unresponsiveness. A drowsy numbness that pains the senses, paradoxical though it may seem, probably has some sound basis in psychological fact; but simply to psychologize the statement without reference to Keats' ideological system will not open the poem to us. It is necessary to see that in the dissolution of ecstasy into heartache and numbness the oxymoronic nature of Keats' ideal has begun to disintegrate into its component parts and that the poet's interpretation of his experience is being distorted by his translation of it into the concepts of the mortal world. What should be thrilling intensity is an intensity of the wrong kind—only the ache of the heart and the pain of the senses; what should be ecstatic selflessness is the wrong kind of selflessness—only drowsy numbness, a slipping Lethe-wards, something comparable to drinking hemlock or a dull opiate. And instead of blending mystically, intensity and selflessness struggle against each other irreconcilably. Ideally, intensities enthrall the self; here the ideal is inverted: numbness pains the sense. In this dichotomy and inversion are contained all the workings of the poem, for the poet's effort to resolve his inner conflict by seeking ease will further split the elements of the poem into tense contrarieties.

—Earl R. Wasserman, *The Finer Tone: Keats' Major Poems* (Baltimore: The Johns Hopkins University Press, 1967): pp. 180–81, 183–85.

⊛

CYNTHIA CHASE ON THE GESTURE OF NAMING FLOWERS

[Cynthia Chase is the editor of *Romanticism* (1993) and the author of *Decomposing Figures: Rhetorical Readings in the Romantic Tradition* (1986) and "Monument and Inscription: Wordsworth's 'Rude Embryo' and the Remains of History" (1990). In the excerpt below from a chapter entitled "Viewless Wings: Keats's *Ode to a Nightingale*," Chase discusses the problem of interpreting the "Ode to a Nightingale," and focuses on the fifth stanza in which the gesture of naming flowers, often read as a casting off of the "viewless wings," is but a questioning of the status of perception.]

The difficulty of interpreting Keats's poetry is closely bound up with its loveliness, its power to gratify our wish for beauty. This is a power to provoke nearly unanimous value judgments together with widely disparate accounts of their occasion. Modern criticism of Keats presents a curious picture: a clear consensus on the harmonious tenor of the development leading from *Sleep and Poetry* to the ode *To Autumn*, together with strong disagreement on the meaning of its individual moments. I will begin by sketching one such disagreement—about how to characterize Keats's situation in the exquisite fifth stanza of the *Ode to a Nightingale*—to help us ask: what investments can we discern here, important enough to be common to such opposite critical readings? For if critics give incompatible accounts of key passages, and yet end with the same judgments, their conclusions must be motivated by some other kind of constraint than the acts of reading from which they ostensibly arise. The nature of such constraints on critical reading can emerge for us, I suggest, if we attend to the tropes and the rhetorical gestures that Keats's ode cites or repeats—if we carry out a certain kind of intertextual reading.

How does one characterize the gesture of the ode's peculiarly Keatsian fifth stanza—naming flowers in the darkness, guessing each sweet, "White hawthorn, and the pastoral eglantine"? It depends on how one reads the fourth: it depends on that notorious crux where—as typically in Keats—the most lovely *and* the most variously interpreted lines of the poem coincide:

> Already with thee! tender is the night,
> > And haply the Queen-Moon is on her throne,
> > > Cluster'd around by all her starry Fays;
>
> > But here there is no light,
> Save what from heaven is with the breezes blown
> > Through verdurous glooms and winding mossy ways.

The fifth stanza continues, "I cannot see what flowers are at my feet. . . ." The question of how to take this passage is loaded by the lines at the opening of stanza 4 with the issue of Keats's commitment to poetic flight:

> Away! away! for I will fly to thee,
> > Not charioted by Bacchus and his pards,
> But on the viewless wings of Poesy,
> > Though the dull brain perplexes and retards:

The decision how to read what follows amounts to a judgment upon the speaker's commitment to "the viewless wings of Poesy." It is here that one finds an incipient consensus, not upon the function of the viewless wings in these lines, but upon the desirability of Keats's ultimately giving them up. Interpretations of the fourth and fifth stanzas converge in a final value judgment—that Keats ought to abandon poetic flight—after diverging widely on just *how* these stanzas mean that. Keats's lines effectively resist attempts to determine the matter more precisely by appealing to them alone, for at this decisive juncture the ode's syntax turns radically ambiguous. To judge the effects of recourse to the viewless wings of poesy we have to decide how to voice the exclamation point after the fourth stanza "thee." A mute mark stands at the place which is *either* an exclamation at arrival or a statement of distance. The punctuation mark doesn't tell us how to hear it: whether as an expression of passionate satisfaction, or as a mere pause for differentiation, like a heavier comma, or displaced italics. To have an *ear* for this can only be to have a stake in a story about the nightingale and Keats. ⟨. . .⟩

More typically this "guessing" of "what flowers are at my feet" is taken as a reward, and as a characteristically Keatsian achievement something like the luxurious surmise of the ode *To Autumn*. Leslie Brisman takes this stanza as a reward for "the demystified *rejection* of transcendent flight" he finds in the fourth stanza. Casting off the "viewless wings" of the visionary imagination together with "the dull brain [that] perplexes and retards" brings Keats at once to the resonant resources "at my feet"—to a "poetry of earth," "to the significant earth whence all sign-constructions take their origin."

We find the same conclusion at the end of an entirely different reading by Jack Stillinger, for whom the speaker's situation in stanza five is not a reward but a bereavement: he sees in it "the speaker's vivid realization of what he has lost by crossing the boundary into an imaginary ideal"—"the transient natural world he has *left behind* and now longs for." Rejection of wings, return to the earth, or adoption of wings, loss of the earth; diametrically opposed as they are, both readings feed into essentially the same account of Keats's accomplishment. He is praised for renouncing finally the Romantic vision of poetry as transcendent flight, and so inaugurating the demystifying gesture of modernism. Critical unanimity about Keats reflects an agreement on how to place Romanticism in the literary tradition. It is seen as a predominantly symbolic and recurrently visionary and escapist mode, to be valued insofar as critical moments of its greatest men, Keats and Wordsworth, anticipate the undeceived modernist vision that marks our own historical moment.

Keats is the poet most assertively invoked where the Romantics are judged from the standpoint of their consistency with a certain note sounded in Stevens and Williams: a "poetry of earth," committed to the intensities and truths of perception. I would suggest that Keats gets invoked in this context because his poetry has to be appropriated, since in fact it *questions* the status of perception, makes the nature of sensory evidence a difficulty. But at the same time Keats's poetry richly gratifies that wish for beauty that impels us to ascribe epistemological authority to the aesthetic, to presume the continuity of perception with knowledge. It is this that makes Keats's texts peculiarly hard to read.

> —Cynthia Chase, *Decomposing Figures: Rhetorical Readings in the Romantic Tradition* (Baltimore: The Johns Hopkins University Press, 1986): pp. 65–67.

☙

KARL P. WENTERSDORF ON THE LITERARY HISTORY OF NIGHTINGALES

[Karl P. Wentersdorf is the author of "Chaucer's Clerk of Oxenford as Rhetorician" (1989) and "The Situation of the Narrator in the Old English Wife's Lament" (1994). In the excerpt below from his article, "The Sub-Text of Keats's 'Ode to a Nightingale,'" Wentersdorf discusses the biographical sub-text of the poem, Keats's love for Fanny Brawne in light of his knowledge of the nightingale's significance in literary history from classical times through the Renaissance.]

It is a commonplace that the greatest poems written by Keats embody the theme of love. Certainly his main preoccupation during the writing of the three long narrative poems published in the volume of 1820 was with the complexity of human love: its ambiguous nature ("Lamia"), its potential for pain and disaster ("Isabella"), and also its potential for ecstatic happiness ("The Eve of St. Agnes"). Enraptured as Keats was by his love for Fanny Brawne, he was not spared the agonies of frustration and jealousy. Since his torments were exacerbated by his weakening physical condition, there were times when he wished to banish love from his life; but it proved impossible to exclude altogether the motif of love from his work.

In the "Ode to a Nightingale," as in the "Ode on a Grecian Urn" and "Ode on Melancholy," Keats is concerned intellectually with the inexorable effects of the passage of time on beauty and on human love. The world of everyday realities is a place of weariness, frustration, and change, "Where beauty cannot keep her lustrous eyes, / Or new Love pine at them beyond to-morrow." What Keats wishes to do is to reach out to a world in which love and beauty are not subject to change. His prime symbol for the imaginative power that will take him on this journey is the nightingale, or more specifically its song.

His excursion in search of that unchanging world, made on "the viewless wings of Poesy," carries him far away from the problems of humanity, out and up into the night sky, yet the trip does not provide him with a vision of an Elysian realm. There is nothing to be perceived, nothing to be recalled in tranquillity and set to paper, because "here there is no light." After the "viewless" excursion is over, all that remains is the memory of the ineffable pleasure given by the nightingale's song. That music, exquisitely melodious at the beginning of the poem and plaintive at the end, calls forth from the underground workshop of the poet's mind a series of images deriving ultimately from ancient times, images that create an emotional sub-text for the poem. Through allusions to the experiences of those who have known the ecstasy of mortal love, Keats reveals his continuing delight at the thought of the joys of young lovers and his deep yearning for the fulfillment of his own unassuaged and incompletely suppressed desires. ⟨. . .⟩

The nightingale was often linked with eros by classical, medieval, and Renaissance writers. It appears in *Paradise Lost* when Adam and Eve withdraw for their wedding night, and all creatures fall silent except for the nightingale singing "all night long her amorous descant"; and it reappears when Milton tells how the primal couple celebrated "the Rites / Mysterious of connubial love" and "lull'd by Nightingales imbracing slept." To Coleridge, the bird's delicious notes were a "love-chant" ("The Nightingale"). Keats's use of this literary tradition is exemplified in *Endymion*, where the nightingale, perched high among the leaves, "sings but to her love," and the summer melody which the bird in "Ode to a Nightingale" sings with "full-throated ease" is a symbol for the passion Keats yearned to be able to express without restraint.

The intimation in stanza 1 that the poem deals in a muted way with the theme of passionate love is supported by the implications of several images later in the poem. Thus stanza 2 contains allusions to manifestations of eros both in classical times and in the Middle Ages. The poet calls for wine, "Tasting of Flora and the country green, / Dance, and Provençal song, and sunburnt mirth!" Flora, whose festival was celebrated in Rome at the end of April and the beginning of May, was a goddess not only of flowers but also of fertility. The festivities of the *Floralia* signalized the annual renewal of life in nature, and they have been variously regarded as joyous revels or as licentious orgies. Ovid, who gives a detailed account of the activities, says that they are marked by wantonness greater than that manifested at other festivals, because Flora warns her devotees to use life's flower while it still blooms, and because the gifts she brings lend themselves to delights. In spite of strong opposition by the Church, the *Floralia* survived through the centuries as "the bringing in of May," and evidence for the enduring popularity of the festival in Britain is provided by the criticism of a sixteenth-century Puritan, by the poetry of Spenser (*Shepheardes Calender* May 20–33), and by the accounts of folklorists.

The traditional association of Flora with the activities of young lovers in the spring is frequently reflected in literature. According to the *Roman de la Rose*, Flora and her husband Zephyrus each year bring forth the flowered counterpanes of the meadows for the encouragement of lovers everywhere. The myth was well known to Spenser, Jonson, and Milton, and Keats himself makes frequent mention of it. Thus in the lyric "O come, dearest Emma!" the "riches of Flora" provide the romantic setting for the persona's "story of love"; in "Sleep and Poetry," the poet envisions the realm "Of Flora, and old Pan" as a place where he can pursue nymphs and "woo sweet kisses," and where one of the nymphs will entice him on "Till in the bosom of a leafy world / We rest in silence."

It is appropriate that in "Ode to a Nightingale" Flora is linked in stanza 2 with the medieval troubadours, for their songs were primarily about those experiences of love that classical writers had associated with Flora and her festival. The love motif in Provençal literature proved to be more than merely a widely imitated literary convention: it helped to disseminate the idea that eros was potentially ennobling for the individual and to set in motion far-reaching changes in society. Although some critics feel skeptical about C. S. Lewis's sweeping statement that the Renaissance itself is "a mere ripple on the surface of literature" compared with the ethical and artistic revolutions which began with the troubadours' praise of human love, it is undeniable that the modern romantic treatment of love in western literature had its origins in Provençal poetry.

—Karl P. Wentersdorf, "The Sub-Text of Keats's 'Ode to a Nightingale,'" *Keats-Shelley Journal* 33 (1984): pp. 70–72, 74.

⚘

FRED V. RANDEL ON THE PROBLEMATIC NATURE OF JOY IN THE POEM

[Fred V. Randel is the author of *The World of Elia: Charles Lamb's Essayistic Romanticism* (1975). In the excerpt below from his article, "Coleridge and the Contentiousness of Romantic Nightingales," Randel discusses Milton's and Coleridge's influence on Keats. He also deals with the problematic nature of joy in terms of the speaker's distress at his participation in the nightingale's happiness.]

The problematics of joy also figures in the most important offspring of Coleridge's debate with Milton: Keats's "Ode to a Nightingale." The month previous to writing it Keats met Coleridge walking on Hampstead Heath and speaking torrentially of a "thousand things," as Keats recalled in a letter, including "Nightingales, Poetry—on Poetical sensation." It was an encounter likely to set the young poet rereading some of Coleridge's poetry, including "The Nightingale." Keats's first stanza addresses the most explicit subject of debate between Coleridge and Milton: the question of whether nightingales are melancholy or joyful. On this issue, Keats is Shakespearean in his inclusiveness. There are, in the first stanza, two levels to the Keatsian synthesis of Milton and Coleridge: first, a human speaker suffers "aches" and "pains" at hearing a nightingale, which enjoys "happiness" and "ease." But this dichotomy is too simple, and a second level is posited: the speaker's distress originates in some share of the nightingale's joy—"being too happy in thine happiness"; that is, getting to know the bird's happiness just well enough to realize how much he is missing. Furthermore, the nightingale's song seems happy in the first stanza, when it can be interpreted as an invitation, but "plaintive" in the last stanza, when the speaker's intervening experiences make him see it as at best lost and at worst delusory. The subject matter of the bird's song likewise shifts from "summer" to death. The perceptions of both Milton and Coleridge are validated but seen as partial. Keats achieves his own originality by making himself an ampler and subtler consciousness, on the first controverted issue, than either Milton or Coleridge, just as his versification outmaneuvers two other predecessors by combining a Shakespearean quatrain with a Petrarchan sestet.

The more fundamental issue raised by Coleridge's poem, however, is whether the organic analogy makes any sense. Keats's great ode tests Coleridge's hypothesis: considering how much value can be found in subtracting from consciousness and trying to approximate nature's preconscious unity with itself. Keats's language of drowsiness, sinking, fading, and forgetting, like Coleridge's language of stretching his limbs, surrendering, and forgetting, renders this subtractive process, the goal of which is a nightingale and, in a word echoing Milton and Coleridge, a "forest *dim*" (emphasis added). Three instruments of subtraction are considered in turn: wine, poesy, and death. The first was probably suggested by Wordsworth's "O Nightingale! thou surely art," which also supplied the idea that a bird's voice could be "buried among trees" (cf. Keats's "and now 'tis buried deep / In the next valley-glades"). Wordsworth, drawing upon Coleridge's "tipsy Joy that reels with tossing head," as well as "The Cuckoo and the Nightingale['s]" association with St. Valentine's Day, takes a step toward Keats's "Bacchus and his pards" when he addresses the nightingale in these words: "Thou sing'st as if the God of wine / Had helped thee to a Valentine. . . ." But Wordsworth is setting a nightingale up in order to put him down, while Keats is investigating the advantages of joining one beneath the trees. So wine, for Keats, conjures up an early stage of the speaker's understanding, rather than a suspicious instability in nightingales. The following stage matters far more because far more emphatically chosen: instead of the ineffectual wishing of "That I might drink," we meet the decisive commitment of "I will fly to thee . . . on the viewless wings of Poesy." The resolution works since "Already with thee!" verbally paralleling "I will fly to thee," indicates that the speaker now imagines himself to be with the nightingale in the forest. It is a long advance in the direction of Coleridge's ideal of uniting the human and the natural, and it is soon followed by the most concretely worded portrayal of nature in the poem, a passage indebted, as Miriam Allott notes in her edition of Keats, to "the dark spring night and its association with growth and renewal in Coleridge's *The Nightingale*."

The same passage, however, is as indebted to Milton as to Coleridge. "I cannot see what flowers are at my feet" reminds us that in Keats's poem, unlike Coleridge's, none of the natural setting can be seen. The speaker is in a world of darkness, like Milton's, whose comments on his own blindness in the invocation to Book III of *Paradise Lost* are several times echoed. Keats's "But here there is no light," beginning the central descriptive passage of the poem, draws on two Miltonic precedents:

> . . . thee I revisit safe,
> And feel thy sovereign vital lamp; but thou
> Revisit'st not these eyes, that roll in vain
> To find thy piercing ray, and find no dawn. . . .

> . . . Thus with the year
> Seasons return, but not to me returns
> Day, or the sweet approach of even or morn. . . .

In all three texts, a renewal or continuance of light before the "but" contrasts with the darkness after it. Keats's descriptive passage is immediately followed by another echo of this invocation: "Darkling I listen" recalls Milton's ". . . as the wakeful bird / Sings darkling, and in shadiest covert hid / Tunes her nocturnal note." The instrument which permits Keats to succeed, momentarily, in attaining a Coleridgean ideal is "the viewless wings of Poesy," which are both invisible and blind—imagination conceived as a secular counterpart to Milton's divinely inspired "celestial Light," which he prays to "Shine inward . . . that I may see and tell / Of things invisible to mortal sight." ⟨. . .⟩

—Fred V. Randel, "Coleridge and the Contentiousness of Romantic Nightingales," *Studies in Romanticism* 21, no. 1 (Spring 1982): pp. 51–53.

⊕

JAMES O'ROURKE ON THE MOVEMENT FROM DAYLIGHT INTO DARKNESS

[James O'Rourke is the author of *Keats's Odes and Contemporary Criticism* (1998) and "'Goody Blake and Harmful Gil,' 'The Thorn' and the Failure of Philanthropy" (1998). In the excerpt below from his article, "Intrinsic Criticism and 'Ode to a Nightingale,'" O'Rourke discusses the structure of the poem as well as the inconsistencies in the critical understanding of the simple movement from daylight into darkness.]

There seems to be a general critical consensus that the Ode begins in full daylight and makes a single movement into darkness; the point is made in such varied commentaries as those of Bush, who says that "The poem had begun in an hour of sunlight. . . . when the poet's imagination has carried him to join the bird in the forest, it is midnight, in a secluded fairy world of sense that is almost cut off from moon and starlight"; Wasserman, whose observation is complicated by a metaphysical apparatus which distinguishes between good and bad darkness and good and bad light in the poem, but who essentially agrees with Bush that "The opening and close of the poem . . . take place in the material world, the soul's daytime"; and Vendler, who senses some logistical difficulty in the movement from daylight to darkness, saying that "The Ode shows signs of improvisation, notably in its passage from a sunlit day to a midnight scene (with no apparent allowance for the passage time)." This point commonly anchors a belief that the Ode is cyclical in structure, in general conformity to M. H. Abrams' description of the "Greater

Romantic Lyric." Abrams does, in fact, say that "Of Keats's odes, that to a Nightingale is the one which approximates the pattern most closely." The cyclical reading implies that when the speaker returns "back from" the nightingale to his "sole self" at the poem's conclusion, he returns to the state in which he began the poem.

While such a reading is structurally satisfying, it is inconsistent with the speaker's own description of his initial identification with the nightingale. In the poem's first stanza, he says that he does not "envy" the nightingale, which would separate him from it, but that he identifies with it; he is "happy in [its] happiness." I would argue that the poem is actually more dialectical than cyclical in its structure, and that there are many more fluctuations and partial shadings of identification between the speaker and the nightingale than can be accounted for in a description of the poem as a single cycle of departure from and return to ordinary experience. The more literal question of time of day in the Ode is complicated by the liberal use in the poem of pathetic fallacy, which blurs interior and exterior landscapes; but perhaps the best reason for doubting that the opening of the poem is meant to convey a sunlit scene is that this is an ode to a nightingale, which is, in the poetic tradition, a bird of the night. The standard poetic association of the nightingale with night includes such well-known material as the daybreak exchange between Romeo and Juliet, where the song of the nightingale functions as the natural sign of the presence of the night.

Wasserman makes both a negative and a positive case for the daylight opening hypothesis, saying that "in stanzas one to three . . . there is no suggestion of darkness," and "In the opening stanza the poet seems able to see the green of the beech trees." But a "plot / Of beechen green and shadows numberless" can slide too easily into "verdurous glooms and winding mossy ways," which is an explicit description of darkness despite the visual potential of "verdurous," "winding," and "mossy," to guarantee that "green" is an actual visual presence and not a poetic locution. The imagery of the poem is at least as dependent on the mood of the speaker as it is on any implied landscape, and descriptive cues can be taken too literally. Wasserman makes the point that the "here" of line 38 (of "here there is no light"), "like the 'Here' of line 24, ["Here, where men sit and hear each other groan"] designates the physical world." While I would say that Wasserman is often overly schematically Platonic, in this case there does seem to be a consistency in the voice of the speaker in which "here" is referred to as a place of spiritual and literal darkness, standing in distinct contrast to an ideal. The contrast is developed in the tableau created of the Queen-Moon and her attendants in the fourth stanza:

> tender is the night,
> And haply the Queen-Moon is on her throne,
> Cluster'd around by all her starry Fays;
> But here there is no light.

"Night," in this image, is a realm of light above the dome of the sky, inhabited by a stellar court, and "here" is the terrestrial world from which one can only surmise what goes on above. The most explicit placement of the speaker in a terrestrial darkness is also an allusion to the Miltonic image of the nightingale and is carried in the word "darkling,"

> the wakeful Bird
> Sings darkling, and, in shadiest Covert hid,
> Tunes her nocturnal Note.
> ⟨*Paradise Lost*⟩

This image anchors the naturalistic placement of the speaker in the night and at the same time invokes the image of the blind bard, deprived of sensory sight but privileged in insight; the passage from Milton occurs in the invocation to light at the beginning of Book Three, where it introduces the poet's lament over his own blindness.

—James O'Rourke, "Intrinsic Criticism and 'Ode to a Nightingale,'" *Keats-Shelley Journal* 37 (1988): pp. 48–50.

⟨꙰⟩

PAUL D. SHEATS ON KEATS'S IMAGINATIVE CONTRIBUTION TO A CLASSICAL GENRE

[Paul D. Sheats is the author of *The Making of Wordsworth's Poetry, 1785–1798* (1973) and the editor of *The Poetical Works of Wordsworth: 1770–1850* (1982). In the excerpt below from his article, "Keats, the Greater Ode, and the Trial of Imagination," Sheats discusses "Ode to a Nightingale" in terms of the status of the ode in the late 18th century, identifying both the ode's classical elements and Keats's imaginative contribution to an ancient poetic genre.]

"The graver and sublimer strains of the Lyric muse," wrote the poet-critic John Aikin in 1772, "are exemplified in the modern ode, a species of composition which admits of the boldest flights of poetical enthusiasm, and the wildest creations of the imagination, and requires the assistance of every figure that can adorn language and raise it above its ordinary pitch." Although Aikin calls it "modern," the enthusiastic decorum he describes clearly belongs to the "greater" ode of the eighteenth century, the richly tangled history of which extends back to antiquity. In the following pages I suggest that several of Aikin's assumptions remained alive into the nineteenth century and that they offer insight into John Keats's attempts to shape a "modern ode." Although Keats's name is linked to the ode because of five poems he composed in 1819, he described eight poems, composed over a span of five years, as "odes," and he probably would have included eight or nine others within a genre that by the early nineteenth century had become capacious and hazily defined. Although neglected by criticism, these "other" odes provide my route of approach to the ode of 1819 most obviously touched by the decorum of the greater ode and its conspicuous invitation to the imagination, the *Ode to a Nightingale*.

Well before Keats came to it, the ode had undergone that leveling and interchange that characterize the traditional genres in the later eighteenth century. In magazines and anthologies, lyrics called "odes" competed with a host of odelike forms: the hymn, effusion, monody, song, and odal sonnet. Critics noted disapprovingly that the ode had dwindled to the level of the song, a view borne out by the confused variety of subjects and manners that appeared under the title of *ode*. The genre might, on a single magazine page, be represented by the Laureate's *Ode for the New Year* and by an *Ode to the Distemper, on Sarella's being taken ill of the Smallpox*.

The traditional outlines of the form nevertheless seem to have survived, at least in the work of the major poets. When Wordsworth pointed to the "transitions" of *Tintern Abbey* and "the passionate music of its versification" as "principal requisites" of the ode, or in his epigraph to the Immortality ode quoted Virgil's allusion to a higher decorum, he invoked the traditional distinction between greater and lesser odes, which Dr. Johnson had defined, in terms of form as well as manner, as a contrast between "sublimity, rapture, and quickness of transition" and "sweetness and ease." ⟨. . .⟩

More particularly, there remained in Keats's time a shared sense of odal decorum, of the form's salient and possibly paradoxical implications. Two such expectations were formal: the sudden transitions mentioned by Johnson, and the vocative mode, which (though not always present) had become, in the absence of other criteria, a generic, indicator. A form traditionally used for public praise, the ode continued to be employed on occasions of national importance. The preferred poetic genre for the celebration of the victories of 1814 and 1815 appears to have been the ode; both Hunt and Keats's friend John Hamilton Reynolds wrote odes on these occasions. Finally, the greater ode continued its association with the creative imagination. The superlatives Aikin bestows on the "modern ode," and his metaphor of "flight," apply as well to the imagination itself, which he describes as an "internal eye" dedicated to the imaging of a new and better world. Modified, sophisticated, and generalized from the ode to poetry, similar assumptions were made by Hazlitt, Hunt, and the young Keats. ⟨. . .⟩

Tradition holds that the first ode to be composed after *Psyche*, in May 1819, was the *Ode to a Nightingale*. If so, this ode constitutes a bravura debut for Keats's new stanza, and it explores a subject matter new to his use of the form—a bird that is at once a natural object and a traditional occasion for lyric apostrophe. The poem also represents a new attempt at fusing the narrative and lyrical modes, an attempt to bring critical judgment to bear on the image-making power that is among Keats's odes formally unique. That *Nightingale* is in some sense a test of the imagination has long been a starting point for criticism; in Stuart Sperry's words, Keats here "tests the possibilities and limits of the creative imagination by confining his attention to a single image, . . . in the effort to endow it with a fullness of identity and the permanence of art." My interest lies in the nature of this "test" and the degree to which it depends on a new, highly dramatic, odal structure, within which the imagination is invoked, objectified, and, at the close, judged. The inventive power Keats had put on "trial" in *Endymion* now enters the genre of the ode as an autonomous character, able, as it were, to fulfill or defeat the expectations of the poet.

For Keats to objectify the imagination is not itself remarkable; such objectification can be said to characterize his view of the creative process. In the act of composition, Richard Woodhouse reported, he took the autonomy of the imagination for granted: imagery "seemed to come by chance or magic—to be as it were something given to me." In a rondeau of January 1819 he had figured Fancy as a tethered bird, able if unleashed to gather pleasures unknown to experience:

> Sit thee there and send abroad,
> With a mind self-overawed,
> Fancy—high commissioned send her!
> . . . .
> She will bring, in spite of frost,
> Beauties that the earth hath lost.
>   (*Fancy*)

Here Keats agrees with Aikin, Hazlitt, and Hunt that a principal function of the imagination is compensatory: its "divineness" consists, as Bacon wrote in a passage cited by Hazlitt in his first lecture of 1818, in its power to alter "the shows of things" on behalf of "the desires of the mind." ⟨. . .⟩

—Paul D. Sheats, "Keats, the Greater Ode, and the Trial of Imagination," in *Coleridge, Keats, and the Imagination: Romanticism and Adam's Dream*, J. Robert Barth, S.J. and John L. Mahoney, eds. (Columbia: University of Missouri Press, 1990): pp. 174–176, 189–190.

Thematic Analysis of
"To Autumn"

Written on September 19, 1819, "To Autumn" is one of Keats's most beautiful and serene poems. Many critics have read it as a statement of Keats's poetic mastery and peaceful celebration of the changes wrought by time and nature. In a letter written to his friend J. H. Reynolds, two days after the poem's composition, Keats spoke of the special warmth and pictorial glow of this season, finding it preferable to "the chilly green of spring." "Somehow a stubble plain looks warm—in the same way that pictures look warm."

Written in the form of the ode, each of the poem's three stanzas appeal to both a particular sensation and a direction of movement. For all its portrayal of abundance and softened sensuality, the poem contains, nevertheless, an unmistakable element of overwhelming satiety. There is also a note of dissimulation and disruption to be found in the same painterly effects that also produce the mood of complete and absolute contentment.

In the **first stanza** of "To Autumn" we get the feeling we are entering into a beautiful and enticing landscape, so adeptly rendered as to disguise the artistic methods through which it achieves its effects, its "[s]eason of mists and mellow fruitfulness." The warmth and assurance of this season is further enhanced by a spirit of loving friendship and benign governance to be found in Nature as we are told that autumn is the "[c]lose bosom-friend of the maturing sun; / Conspiring with him to load and bless / With fruit." Indeed, the first stanza is a veritable cornucopia, a curved horn overflowing with fruits and grain used as a decorative device, which is emblematic of abundance and inexhaustible provision. We feel the weight of fruitfulness as it is Nature's intention "[t]o bend with apples the moss'd cottage-trees, / And fill all fruit with ripeness to the core." Yet for all of the "swell[ing] of the gourd" and "plump[ing] of the hazel shells," we are very aware of an acknowledged deception taking place within the artistic framework of overflowing abundance: after all, autumn marks the transition between the warmth of summer and the barrenness of winter. Thus, it is merely an illusion that the season will endlessly "set budding more, / And still more," and only the bees will be deceived by this scene of plenitude and complete sufficiency: "Until they think warm days will never cease, / For summer has o'er-brimm'd their clammy cells."

In the **second stanza**, the poet addresses autumn as if it were a human presence. In so doing, he utilizes the rhetorical device of apostrophe (which in its Greek origin means "to turn away"). Apostrophe is a figure of speech that addresses an absent or dead person or thing, or even an abstract idea, as if it were alive and present and understood what was being said. Additionally, the term originally meant an abrupt turning away from the normal audience to address a more specific and different one. Here, in this second stanza, Keats has turned away from the reader of the first stanza in order to speak directly to autumn: "Who hath not seen thee oft amid thy store?"

Several images and additional poetic procedures follow, all conveying the tensions within the poem as the illusion of fullness and completion is laden with contradiction. We do not even get a clear or fully satisfying delineation of the figure of autumn, as we are told that autumn is not always responsible: "Sometimes whoever seeks abroad may find / Thee sitting careless on a granary floor." Nevertheless, he is always endearing, and equally vulnerable to the illusions of the season he represents, intoxicated by the scene he both creates and in which he participates: "Thy hair soft-lifted by the winnowing wind; / Or on a half-reap'd furrow sound asleep, / Drows'd with the fume of poppies."

The word "winnow," from the Old English *windwian*, which meant "to fan," can mean to remove the chaff from the grain by a current of air or, more generally, to get rid of something undesirable. This word introduces yet another tension within this season of ripeness and satiety. Keats's autumn functions as both reaper, cutting down the grain with his scythe, and gleaner, gathering up the grain after the reaper has played his part. Thus, "To Autumn" now implies both abundance and sacrifice; the season can be both benevolent and ruthless. "While thy hook / Spares the next swath and its twined flowers: / And sometimes like a gleaner thou dost keep / Steady thy laden head across a brook." Here, autumn prefers to be lazy and abdicate his responsibility, watching, "by a cyder-press, with patient look, . . . the last oozings hours by hours." Autumn chooses to succumb to the illusion that time stands still, preferring to forget that his season is but a brief moment.

In the **third stanza**, the poet turns away from directly addressing autumn, and returns to the reader whom he addressed in the first stanza. This time, though, the perspective on this season of absolute fulfillment is far more uncertain. Keats begins this last stanza as a question, "Where are the songs of spring? Ay, where are they?" Immediately thereafter, he becomes defensive about his perspective: "Think not of them, thou hast thy music too."

We come now to a far more rhetorically violent gesture; Keats must banish Spring and its beautiful music and replace it with a far different song. "Then in a wailful choir the small gnats mourn / Among the river sallows, borne aloft / Or sinking as the light wind lives or dies." The music that replaces the sweet songs of spring can be harsh and jarring to the ear, as "full-grown lambs loud bleat from hilly bourn" or even barely audible as "now with treble soft / The red-breast whistles from a garden-croft." Indeed, these images of sorrow and death in the natural world are harbingers of the bleak season that is to follow, symbols of the undeniable mortality of the poet. ❁

Critical Views on
"To Autumn"

HERMIONE DE ALMEIDA ON THE TENSIONS OF THE SEASON

[Hermione de Almeida is the author of "Pharmacy in Keats's 'Ode on Melancholy'" (1987), *Romantic Medicine and John Keats* (1991) and "Prophetic Extinction and the Misbegotten Dream in Keats" (1998). In the excerpt below from her book, de Almeida discusses "To Autumn" as Keats's "final, diagnostic reading of life," a reading in which the abundance of the season is continually undermined by images of confusion, anxiety, and transience.]

Keats's last and perhaps most perfect ode, "To Autumn," provides the pattern and the sign to the poet's final, diagnostic reading of life.

> Season of mists and mellow fruitfulness,
>   Close bosom-friend of the maturing sun;
> Conspiring with him how to load and bless
>   With fruit the vines that round the thatch-eves run;
> To bend with apples the moss'd cottage-trees,
>   And fill all fruit with ripeness to the core;
>   To swell the gourd, and plump the hazel shells
> With a sweet kernel; to set budding more,
> And still more, later flowers for the bees,
> Until they think warm days will never cease,
>   For summer has o'er brimm'd their clammy cells.

The ripened life of autumn's harvest is a compound potion of tangible substance and intangible illusion. The poet would have us read between the rows of "gold autumn's whole kingdoms of corn" ("Apollo to the Graces,") and ponder whether the picture of autumn's harvest represents a process of abundancy and maturation, as it should, or whether it is an illusory excess summoned in the face of finitude. Autumn's brief bounty is clearly suspect from the start. The season of mellow fruitfulness and distinct substantial creation is also a season of disorienting mists that chill the body, confuse the senses, blur the lines of physical existence, and provoke the anxieties of rational consciousness. The inductive warmth of autumn makes it an unlikely—and perhaps too close—"bosom-friend" of the maturing and therefore wintry sun. Sun and season together conspire for mutual benefit (much as Hermes and Lamia did in *Lamia*): they seduce with pain and pleasure, loading and blessing vine, tree, and blossoming plant until nature fruits and flowers simultaneously as an unearthly paradise removed from mortal time. Autumn's activity to "swell the gourd, and plump the hazel shells" is a pressure, an ambivalent physical sensation reminiscent of, as Ricks describes it, "the pressure of sleep and of opiate"; its overweening need to "fill all fruit with ripeness to the core" prompts the realization meanwhile that at the core physical life disintegrates first. In the never-never land of *Endymion*'s sea palace, a parallel superabundance prevailed:

> Nectar ran
> In courteous fountains to all cups outreach'd;
> And plunder'd vines, teeming and exhaustless, pleach'd
> New growth about each shell and pendant lyre.

But there the fantasy was real, at least for the dead lovers who are "reanimated" from their icy tombs at the stroke of a dreaming poet's wand. Here, in the seasonal world of Keats's maturity, nothing teems exhaustless and the bees and flowers are autumn's fools. We are to read in autumn's ability to mimic and outdo the summer in fostering life, in its ability to set flowers "budding more, /And still more" and to make the bees "think warm days never cease," a cruel and illusory excess of life. The "hurry and alarm / When the bee-hive casts its swarm" upon hearing "the autumn breezes sing" of winter ("Fancy") presages the "frozen time" of drear-nighted December: sleety thawings will glue the flower buds, summer's overbrimming honey will congeal around the larvae, and some juveniles will not grow wings and instead rot at the core of the hive.

Life is *too* much in late autumn, and a harvest is always ambiguous. We are reminded of the premature harvest forced forth to honor Pan in Book I of *Endymion* when the fig trees foredoom their fruit, the yellow bees surrender the sweetness and larvae of their "golden honeycombs," the overexcited butterflies give up their "freckled wings," and the chuckling linnet abandons "its five young unborn / To sing" for the indifferent Pan; the forced growth of this scene finds further, unnatural parallel in a subsequent harvest scene when nature is overripe: "deepest shades" turn "deepest dungeons," "heaths and sunny glades" fill with "pestilential light," "taintless rills" seem "sooty, and o'er-spread with upturned gills / Of dying fish," and the "vermeil rose" is overblown "In frightful scarlet" with "its thorns out-grown / Like spiked aloe." Premature and too-late harvests in the early poetry anticipate yet another vision of ripeness where the harvest turns out to be only an anticipated harvest born of the fears of a "teeming brain": the poet's vision of "high piled books, in charactry" holding "like rich garners the full-ripen'd grain" of his aspirations, all harvest shadows dissipated by "the magic hand of chance" and preempted by the premonitions of real death ("When I have fears"). This autumnal harvest of poetic achievement seen as horrific unfulfillment by a young and dying poet, in turn, reminds us of the "feast of summer fruits" that the poet of *The Fall of Hyperion* tastes and knows on closer inspection to be not an immortal cornucopia but picnic leavings abandoned by the gods— the "refuse of a meal." These harvests foreshadow and foredoom autumn's leavings in an ode that is no ode and, certainly, no picnic.

Within autumn's seasonal illusion of life as abundance and fruitful excess, as pictured in stanza 1 of "To Autumn," can be found mute promise of autumn's minimal life, a shallow bounty of gnats, crickets, and twittering swallows summoned briefly to life and or activity by the sad music of stanza 3. Autumn's harvest beauty, a process or procession of sacrifice like that graven on the Grecian urn of Keats's other ode to life, is dependent upon the experience of transience. It is a passing pleasure felt through the pain or knowledge of what follows after the illusion of boundless or eternal life fades. ⟨. . .⟩

Life, for Keats, is the ebbing of life. What the physician saw in the clinic for the terminally ill—a specific exhaustion of mortal life that could not be stopped by any medicine and a general wanton display of the ebbing of finite energy in mankind—was the very same thing that the poet envisioned in nature at large. Both kinds of healers read life through the advanced perceptual lenses of their various disciplines, and their readings of life's "leavings" proved to be identical: life was the sight and the sign of its painful depletion. In a Romantic age that had made life the primary subject of inquiry and generated numerous and conflicting testimonials on the nature of life, Keats's portrait of life in autumn stands at the point of consensus on the subject among the physiologists and philosophers of his time. All would acknowledge that life, invisible until the moment of "first flush," could only be known at ebb, and all would agree that the life force revealed itself in the physical world of creatures through the debilitating albeit generative windings down of its own finite energies.

—Hermione de Almeida, *Romantic Medicine and John Keats* (New York: Oxford University Press, 1991): pp. 312–14, 319.

⊗

MARK BRACHER ON ABUNDANCE AND FULFILLMENT

[Mark Bracher is the author of *Lacan, Discourse, and Social Change: A Psychoanalytic Cultural Criticism* (1993) and *The Writing Cure: Psychoanalysis, Composition, and the Aims of Education* (1999). In the excerpt below from his article, "Ideology and Audience Response to Death in Keats's 'To Autumn,'" Bracher challenges two prevailing critical foundations: that the poem is an objective description of reality and that its theme is death. He focuses instead on its images of abundance and fulfillment, as well as its acceptance of mortality.]

Few short romantic poems have received more positive response from readers than Keats's "To Autumn." Among contemporary critics, Christopher Ricks pronounces it "the greatest of Keats's odes," Geoffrey Hartman finds it to be without defect, and Harold Bloom declares it to be a "perfect poem," or at least "as close to perfection as any shorter poem in English." Such superlatives indicate that these readers find the poem deeply gratifying in some way. Other readers are more explicit about this gratification, testifying that the poem satisfies the very core of their desire. For Walter Jackson Bate, the poem offers "what the heart really wants" (Bloom agrees); for Anne Mellor, the poem leads readers to feel, "We have had enough"; and for Paul Fry the poem produces "the suspension of desire."

What is particularly significant about this response is that it is produced by a poem usually thought to have two features that would

8

seem to preclude such feelings of fulfillment. First, the poem is often said to be an objective description of reality, completely free of mystification, wish-fulfillment, or tendentiousness of any kind, and second, the poem is thought by most to be fundamentally about death (a somewhat paradoxical claim itself, *prima facie*, since death nowhere figures as an explicit topic in the poem). In short, the consensus has been that the poem provides a powerful experience of fulfillment, that it does so by describing a natural scene, in which death figures prominently, and that this description somehow brings readers to an acceptance of their own mortality. In Richard Macksey's view, the poem "calmly accepts emptiness and death"; for Mellor the poem is permeated by "a willed acceptance of the contradictions of human experience, of the chaotic infinity of nature, and of human mortality"; and for Bloom the poem offers "an image of natural death as an imaginative finality, a human consummation to be wished, though not devoutly."

Ideology in "To Autumn"

But how, one might ask, can a poem that simply "accepts" what is given—a poem which "demands nothing, claims nothing, insists on nothing, contains nothing to dispute about, praises no one, attacks no one, [and] never once reflects upon itself"—how can such a poem produce an acceptance of death which, moreover, is experienced as a deep fulfillment? The answer, of course, is that it cannot; and in the past decade several critics, beginning with Geoffrey Hartman, have observed a number of ways in which the poem's apparent disinterestedness and objectivity are in fact illusory, and "that ['To Autumn'] is an ideological poem." One aspect of the poem's ideology has been indicated by Donald Pearce, who notes that Keats is being quite selective in the poem—e.g., no one is shown doing any work—and that "under even the simplest natural description there is bound to lie some metaphysical bedrock—something in virtue of which certain attitudes toward a scene (hence certain values) are celebrated and others excluded (or even, by implication, opposed)." Jerome McGann, declaring that "the poem is not impersonal, [that] it is tendentious and ideological in quite specific ways," observes that the poem's special effect is to remove the fearful aspects of these themes [of living and dying, maturing and decaying, staying and leaving] to make us receive what might otherwise be threatening ideas in the simpler truth of certain forms which the poet presents as images of The Beautiful. This effect is produced by so manipulating the mythological and artistic mediations that the reader agrees to look at autumn, and to contemplate change and death, under certain precise and explicitly fictional guises. The reader accepts the invitation because these mediations, though recognizably fictional, nevertheless promise a real human benefit: the beauty of the mediations can transform one's felt response to the ideas of change, death, decay. Keats's poem is itself proof that such historically generated fictions, self-consciously embraced, can have this consoling power.

Despite their recognition of various ideological elements, however, these critics do not pursue the deeper ramifications of the poem's ideological force. In fact, they tend to repress their own acknowledgement of the ideological nature of the poem. ⟨. . .⟩

A major reason for this oblivion of the ideological lies in the fact that these critics implicitly identify ideology with a discrepancy between description and fact, between representation and the actual events of history. This view of ideology, and the results of this view for criticism, find their clearest articulation in McGann's statement that "the poem's autumn is a historically specified fiction dialectically called into being by John Keats as an active response to, and alteration of, the events which marked the late summer and early fall of a particular year in a particular place. Keats's poem is an attempt to 'escape' the period which provides the poem with its context, and to offer its readers the same opportunity of refreshment." ⟨. . .⟩

The fundamental problem, then, with the ideological analyses of the poem to date, is that even when critics have recognized "To Autumn" as ideological, they have failed to apprehend the true locus of ideology. Contrary to their assumption, ideology cannot be located in the distortion or elision, per se, of certain facts or events. It must be sought, rather, in the effects that such distortion and elision (and other factors as well) produce in human subjects. As Althusser reminds us, "there is no ideology except by the subject and for subjects . . . [since] all ideology has the function (which defines it) of constituting concrete individuals as subjects." The ideology of a poem thus resides not in the distortion or elision of facts or events

but in what Althusser has called the interpellation of the subject—
i.e., in those aspects of the poem that produce a certain (dis)position
of the reading subject. ⟨...⟩

—Mark Bracher, "Ideology and Audience Response to Death in
Keats's 'To Autumn,'" *Studies in Romanticism* 29, no. 4 (Winter 1990):
pp. 633–36, 639.

Ⓢ

WALTER JACKSON BATE ON THE LITERARY PERFECTION OF THE POEM

[Walter Jackson Bate is the author of *From Classic to
Romantic: Premises of Taste in Eighteenth Century England*
(1946), *John Keats* (1963), and *The Burden of the Past and
the English Poet* (1970). In the excerpt below from his
biography of Keats, Bate discusses "To Autumn" in terms of
the critical commonplace that it is "one of the most nearly
perfect poems in English" and attributes that appeal to its
offering many different types of resolution.]

It is because "To Autumn" is so uniquely a distillation, and at many
different levels, that each generation has found it one of the most
nearly perfect poems in English. We need not be afraid of
continuing to use the adjective. In its strict sense the word is
peculiarly applicable: the whole is "perfected"—carried through to
completion—solely by means of the given parts; and the parts
observe decorum (for no other poem of the last two centuries does
the classical critical vocabulary prove so satisfying) by contributing
directly to the whole, with nothing left dangling or independent.
The "Ode to a Nightingale," for example, is a less "perfect" though a
greater poem. The distinctive appeal of "To Autumn" lies not merely
in the degree of resolution but in the fact that, in this short space, so
many different kinds of resolution are attained.

Most of what Keats had developed in the structure of the ode
stanza the previous April and May reappears effortlessly now (the
poem seems to have been written easily). There is only one new
variation, simple but altogether appropriate: the ode stanza is given
a more prolonged effect; and the prolonging of fulfillment is itself an

intrinsic part of the theme of the ode. Not only the formal structure but the whole conception of the odal hymn becomes transparent before its subject. The poet himself is completely absent; there is no "I," no suggestion of the discursive language that we find in the other odes; the poem is entirely concrete, and self-sufficient in and through its concreteness. But if dramatic debate, protest, and qualification are absent, it is not because any premises from which they might proceed are disregarded but because these premises are being anticipated and absorbed at each step. The result (in contrast to the "Nightingale" or the "Grecian Urn") is also a successful union of the ideal—of the heart's desire—and reality; of the "greeting of the Spirit" and its object. What the heart really wants is being found (in the first stanza, fullness and completion; in the second, a prolonging of that fulfillment). Here at last is something of a genuine paradise, therefore. It even has its deity—a benevolent deity that wants not only to "load and bless" ("conspiring" with its friend, the sun), but also to "spare," to prolong, to "set budding more." And yet all this is put with concrete exactness and fidelity.

These resolutions are attained partly through still another one to which Keats's poetry has so often aspired: a union of process and stasis (or what Keats had called "stationing"). Each of the three stanzas concentrates on a dominant, even archetypal, aspect of autumn, but, while doing so, admits and absorbs its opposite. The theme of the first is ripeness, of growth now reaching its climax beneath the "maturing sun," as the strain of the weighty fruit bends the apple trees and loads the vines. The cells of the beehives are already brimming over. Yet growth is still surprisingly going on, as autumn and the sun conspire "to set budding more, / And still more, later flowers," and as the bees are deceived into feeling that summer will never end:

> Season of mists and mellow fruitfulness,
>   Close bosom-friend of the maturing sun;
> Conspiring with him how to load and bless
>   With fruit the vines that round the thatch-eves run;
> To bend with apples the moss'd cottage-trees,
>   And fill all fruit with ripeness to the core;
>   To swell the gourd, and plump the hazel shells
>   With a sweet kernel; to set budding more,
> And still more, later flowers for the bees,
> Until they think warm days will never cease,
>   For Summer has o'er-brimm'd their clammy cells.

If, in the first stanza, we find process continuing within a context of stillness and attained fulfillment, in the second—which is something of a reverse or mirror image of the first—we find stillness where we expect process. For now autumn is conceived as a reaper or harvester. Yet it is a harvester that is not harvesting. This benevolent deity is at first motionless, "sitting careless on a granary floor," or asleep on a "half-reap'd furrow," while its "hook / Spares the next swath and all its twined flowers"—spares not only the full grain but those new "later flowers" that are interlocking with it. Movement begins only in the latter part of the stanza. Even then it is only suggested in the momentary glimpses of the figure of the gleaner keeping "steady" its "laden head" as it crosses a brook; and autumn then stops again to watch the slow pressing of the apples into cider as the hours pass: ⟨. . .⟩

There is a hint that the end is approaching—these are the "last oozings"—and the pervading thought in what follows is the withdrawal of autumn, the coming death of the year, and of course the familiar archetypal relevance of the association to our feelings of sequence in our own lives. But if the conception in the previous stanzas has been carried out partly through contrary images—fulfilled growth, while growth still continues; the reaper who is not reaping— the procedure now is almost completely indirect and left solely to inference. The personified figure of autumn is replaced by concrete images of life, and of life unafflicted by any thought of death: the gnats, the hedge crickets, the redbreast. Moreover, it is life that can exist in much the same way at other times than autumn. ⟨. . .⟩

—Walter Jackson Bate, *John Keats* (Cambridge, Mass.: The Belknap Press of Harvard University Press, 1963): pp. 581–83.

⟨ॐ⟩

DONALD PEARCE ON DISTURBANCE AND INTERRUPTION IN THE POEM

[Donald Pearce is an editor of *Blake in His Time* (1978) and *Para/worlds: Entanglements of Art and History* (1989). In the excerpt below from his article, "Thoughts on the Autumn Ode of Keats," Pearce discusses the tensions within the poem. The poem at first appears to be a celebration of the abundance of the season, yet simultaneously it contains elements of disturbance and interruption.]

It is, of course, a superb "Landscape," in the opinion of some the finest in the language, a poem of almost pure description. ⟨...⟩

A rich autumn landscape, done by a youthful poet of love and nature, in an apparently happy frame of mind. The most innocent-looking of poems. Which of course it is, though at the same time is not—for the "rich autumn landscape" isn't the only poem that is here. One soon becomes aware of a second poem, just below the surface of the familiar one, a poem so intent, so looming, so full of wonder, that you almost hold your breath reading it. This under poem, or inner poem, is the one I want to consider in these notes. Parts of it can be seen immediately, registered here and there at the surface, so to speak, of the outer poem as a visible disturbance in the syntax. The ode opens in fact with an instance of this, where in spite of the stanza's appearance of weight and calm there is plainly enough emotional stress occurring somewhere below the surface of the lines to disrupt the grammatical structure of the stanza and produce not the completed thought or statement one had expected but an interrupted, suspended, eleven line sentence-fragment instead. It is a great opening certainly, and wonderfully dramatic: in the very act of reading it, the stanza changes from quiet descriptive statement, to exclamation, to sustained apostrophe, almost requiring of the reader a triple take. And then the calm fashion in which Keats manages this piece of virtuosity, with all the confidence in the world trailing that salutation out over a succession of present infinitives (six of them!) like a vine over a series of vine props, or like the season's own quiet succession of warm afternoons: "Season of mists . . . conspiring how . . . to load . . . to bless . . . to fill . . . to swell . . . to plump . . . to set budding. . . ." You wonder if it is ever going to end, but end it does, to break off abruptly and hang suspended in mid air, till engaged by the waiting "Who hast not seen thee . . . ?" of the next stanza, where it is not fully resolved either, final resolution not really occurring till the "Thou-hast-thy-music-too" section far down the ode in stanza three. The main rhetorical schema of the ode would then be reducible to something like: *Season of mists . . . Who has not seen thee? . . . Heard thee?* . . . upon which simple triadic framework Keats mounts a thirty-three line salute to the autumn season that for fugal duration of tone and cadence must surely be the equal of anything in the work of his admired Spenser or Milton.

⟨. . .⟩ Those critics who have commented on its structure, if they haven't always been in agreement as to its exact form have at least agreed that it is basically consecutive, the stanzas moving in orderly sequence, like a piece of music from the opening apostrophe, through the great personifications, to the quiet benediction of the close. And there is discernible progress also, as has often been noted, in the early→ to middle→ to late autumn imagery (which would hardly have been unintentional on Keats's part). But I believe there is another principle of order in this poem than sequentiality, taking priority over sequence because more in harmony with the deeper concerns of the poem, viz. that of a *contemplation*. As I understand this special mental state, its distinguishing quality is that it is "plotless," non-directional, without appetency; it is static attention, attention without progress.

That "To Autumn" more resembles a contemplation than a narrative (or pictorial) sequences became clear the moment I saw that the various presented events, though they may be followed consecutively, have in fact no "necessary" connections with each other. That is to say, they are joined not by any logical plot or argument but simply *by the fact of taking place*. Not that the vines, flowers, birds, fields form only a loose collage; they exhibit more design and coherence than that—a contemplation, after all, is not a jumble. I mean, instead, that it is by accumulation rather than by progression of effects, by co-presence rather than by sequence, that they are able to *become* Autumn in the end.

> —Donald Pearce, "Thoughts on the Autumn Ode of Keats," *Ariel* 6, no. 3 (July 1975): pp. 3–6.

ⓢ

PATRICK SWINDEN ON THE SEASON OF ACHIEVEMENT IN THE POEM

[Patrick Swinden is the author of *Silas Marner: Memory and Salvation* (1992) and *Literature and the Philosophy of*

Intention (1999). In the excerpt below from his article, "John Keats: 'To Autumn,'" Swinden analyzes the poem in terms of Keats's requirement that great poetry contains both power and ease. Swinden concludes that autumn in this poem symbolizes a season of achievement and mature fulfillment.]

In one of his letters Keats says that 'the excellence of every Art is its intensity'; in another that poetry should come 'as naturally as leaves to a tree' or it should not come at all. When critics say, as they often do, that 'To autumn' is his most perfect poem, they probably mean that in it Keats's two requirements of great poetry, power and ease, are held in exact equilibrium. The poetry is then, as Keats said it should be, 'great and unobtrusive'. I think this is as nearly true here as it could ever be, and so I see my task in discussing 'To autumn' as one of explaining how, in this poem, Keats realised his high and difficult ambition.

The poem doesn't *sound* as if it has been strenuously worked at. It has a simplicity of development, a quality of *unfolding*, that makes its movement seem inevitable; almost as if nobody could be expected to write about autumn in any other way. And much of the evidence points to the conclusion that Keats did indeed write the poem with little strain or difficulty. This is true even of the second stanza (probably the last in order of composition), which was the most heavily revised.

It is a fact, nevertheless, that Keats misses out of this poem altogether one of the two most conspicuous aspects of an English, or for that matter any other, autumn. The gathering of the harvest is there, in a wealth of beautifully modulated detail. But where are the falling, or fallen, leaves? Remembering Thomas Hood's 'Autumn' ('Where is the pride of Summer,—the green prime,— / The many many leaves all twinkling?') or Gerard Manley Hopkins's 'Spring and fall,' and a host of other poems on the subject of autumn, we ought to find this surprising; and it is a tribute to Keats that in reading his poem we ignore such a gaping hole at the centre of his treatment of its subject. I think it is important to our understanding of the poem that we ask ourselves why Keats has omitted the falling leaves, and how it is that we fail to notice he has done so. ⟨. . .⟩

Isn't the explanation more intimately concerned with the underlying theme of the poem, and Keats's unconventional treatment of it? The fact is that in poems, and often in novels and other works of art, falling leaves are not just falling leaves: they are metaphors of sadness, of grief perhaps (as in Hopkins's 'Margaret, are you grieving / Over goldengrove unleaving?'), or at any rate of the end of some phase of vitality which must now pause—for ever, or to be resumed in the new year, in the spring (as in Shakespeare's 'That time of year, thou may'st in me behold / When yellow leaves, or none, or few, do hang . . .'). ⟨. . .⟩ The autumn that we are responding to is very much out there, an objective fact that is being recorded by the poet, rather than a metaphorical substitute for a cry of sadness at the pain of living and the mortality of man. ⟨. . .⟩

I can explain my attitude best by recalling the absence of dead leaves, and applying it to a reading of the ending of the poem. Here, the poet suggests the coming of winter by describing the gathering swallows twittering in the skies. An astute critic of Keats has suggested that since we know Keats studied the Latin poet Virgil at school, in some detail, he might have had at the back of his mind here a passage from the sixth book of the *Aeneid* which describes the souls of the dead waiting on the banks of the river Styx to be ferried into the Underworld. ⟨. . .⟩ If this were in Keats's mind and if he managed to convey it into the poem, it would certainly produce a strong impression of death and decay as the inevitable conclusion of autumn. But it is significant that *if* Keats had the passage from the *Aeneid* in mind, then for some reason he omitted the image that preceded the bird (not 'swallows' specifically) image in Virgil— namely the image of the dead being 'thick as the leaves in the forest that at autumn's first frost dropping fall'. So Keats's image of the swallows, which 'gather' but do not 'flock shoreward, when the chill of the year drives them overseas,' carries at best the light suggestion of Vergilian pathos, combining with the earlier description of mourning gnats 'borne aloft or sinking as the light wind lives or dies' to hint in the gentlest, the least despondent way, at the decline of the season into the death of winter.

I am suggesting that Keats is aware of the fact that autumn heralds the coming of winter, and therefore of all that we associate with death; but that in writing his poem about autumn he chooses to dwell most fully on the season as a time of achievement, of a mature fruition. This is so much the case that in the first stanza he seems to suggest that whatever potential, as distinct from actuality, autumn displays, is a potential for replenishment, a reaching out across a forgotten winter to the renewal of spring: 'to set budding more, / And still more, later flowers for the bees . . .'. Elsewhere the emphasis often falls on a movement that has been arrested, the harvester sound asleep on his half reaped furrow, the gleaner keeping steady her laden head across a brook. It is as if autumn has become a condition of rest, in which the pressure of time, hastening season into season, has been converted into a pressure of a different kind, a pressure that loads, bends, fills, swells and plumps the fruit, the apples, the gourds and the hazel nuts.

—Patrick Swinden, "John Keats: 'To Autumn,'" *Critical Quarterly* 20, no. 4 (Winter 1978): pp. 57–59.

JUHANI RUDANKO ON THE NEVER-ENDING PROCESS OF NATURE AND HUMAN LIFE

[Juhani Rudanko is the author of *Change and Continuity in the English Language: Studies on Complementation Over the Past Three Hundred Years* (1998). In the excerpt below from the article, "Activity as Process in *To Autumn*," Rudanko conducts a close, literal reading of the "language" of the poem in terms of the never-ending process of Nature and the maturing of human life.]

The methodological perspective adopted here supports a more literal and a less "mythic" reading of the poem than has been the case in a number of relatively recent studies. Among such studies arguing for mythic implications of the poem is that by S. R. Swaminathan. However, it is with refreshing and comforting candor that he states that "the poem does not explicitly refer to any myths. . . ." In this respect the poem differs from some others by Keats, but this difference may only have contributed to its enduring appeal, especially these days when interest in, and knowledge of, mythology has been on the decline.

The first stanza opens with two noun phrases. Autumn is (the) season of mists and mellow fruitfulness and (a) close bosom-friend of the maturing sun. Autumn conspires with the sun to do many things, expressed—apart from the last—by a series of verb phrases which exhibit a high degree of parallelism, as emphasized by Donald Freeman: to load and bless the vines with fruit, to bend the moss'd cottage trees with apples, to fill all fruit with ripeness to the core, to swell the gourd, to plump the hazel shells with a sweet kernel and to set budding more and later flowers for the bees until they think that warm days will never cease.

The stanza is dominated by the related notions of maturing and mellowness. To mature is to become mature or to cause to become mature. The ambiguity is inherent in the *maturing sun*, as has been observed. The stanza is dominated thematically by adjectives and verb constructions which are more or less closely linked in meaning: *mellow, load with fruit, fill with ripeness, swell, plump with a kernel.* In addition to syntactic parallelism, there is a pattern of meaningful semantic recurrence. The adjective *soft* is less closely connected with maturing but is related in a broader sense, especially by way of the adjective *mellow.* (It is instructive to consider the seven senses of the adjective *mellow* in the OED. In five of the seven, *soft* or a derivative of *soft* appears.) It occurs once in the second stanza and twice in the third stanza, contributing to the thematic content and coherence of the poem.

In the first stanza autumn is anthropomorphized. In the second stanza it is more clearly personified. However, the poem stops short of saying whether the figure of autumn is male or female. In order not to have to refer to the figure by the pronoun *it,* which seems inappropriate for a personified figure, a female figure will be assumed here. Possible sources of inspiration for the second stanza, as discussed by Jack and Davenport, i.a., tend to support the view that the figure is female. However, such considerations are necessarily extrinsic to the poem and cannot therefore be decisive.

The second stanza details four spatial locations where the personified figure of autumn may be found: sitting on a granary floor, careless, on a half reaped furrow, soundly asleep while her hook spares the next swath, carrying a load on her head across a brook and watching the last oozings of a cyder-press.

The third stanza provides a description of the music of autumn. The music, located temporally first by *while* and *then* and later by *now*, is of different kinds: the small gnats mourn in a wailful choir, full-grown lambs bleat, hedge-crickets sing, the red-breast whistles in a soft treble, and gathering swallows twitter. The stubble plains constitute the spatial locations for this music, but the sounds issue from different places: the bleating of lambs from a hilly bourn, the whistling of redbreast from a garden-croft and the twittering of swallows from the skies.

The setting of the ode points to the central image of the stubble plains. To quote Vendler: "The whole poem, to my mind, is uttered from the stubble-plains. . . ." Vendler's statement is perhaps something of a hyperbole, for it is difficult to maintain that the first and second stanzas are uttered from the stubble plains. If this quibble is set aside, it is possible to agree with her that the image is crucial in the third stanza and important in the whole poem. However, Vendler's interpretation of the symbolic value of this central image is in some ways difficult to accept and will be challenged here. She suggests that the stubble plains imply deprivation, arguing that the tones of the poem, "even of greatest celebration, are, I think, intelligible only when they are heard as notes issuing from deprivation." ⟨. . .⟩

The key sentence here is the statement "a stubble plain looks warm." The statement is impressive and powerful in its simplicity. As Jugurtha puts it: "There is no melancholic mood or hint of death in the letter. . . . Even today one may have a feeling of warmth when walking in a stubble field on a mild autumn day and it is a feeling of warmth that the letter conveys, especially regarding the force of the central image of the stubble field. ⟨. . .⟩

The ode is about the season of autumn, and, in a transferred sense, about the age of maturity in the life of a human being. The present interpretation privileges the large number of processes, acts and events that take place at this season. Dying is recognized in the poem as one of these, but the poem does not contemplate autumn and the age of maturity primarily as seasons of desolation or of blankness when processes, actions and events are completed, finished and then dead. Rather, the poem is lighter and warmer. It celebrates autumn and the age of maturity as seasons when a very large number of processes and actions are in progress. Many of the processes and actions are dynamic. And some of them are languorously suspended, others are more intense, even to the point of fusion. Overall, such variety of "never-ceasing" process and activity denotes richness, not death and desolation.

—Juhani Rudanko, "Activity as Process in *To Autumn*," *Language and Style* 24, no. 3 (Summer 1991): pp. 316–18, 321.

ⓝ

Thematic Analysis of
"La Belle Dame Sans Merci:
A Ballad"

Written on April 21, 1819, and published in 1820, the title of the poem, "La Belle Dame Sans Merci: A Ballad," was taken from a medieval poem by Alain Chartier. The French title means "The Lovely Lady without Pity," and the ballad tells the story of a mortal destroyed by his love for a supernatural femme fatale.

As a genre, ballads are typically short, highly dramatic poems that originated in folk tradition; at one time they were transmitted orally among illiterate people. The ballad's most common themes include vampirism, violence, and eroticism; they are often set in strange and gloomy surroundings, such as haunted castles full of magic spells and treacherous ladies. All of these details bear a strong resemblance to the medieval romance. The ballad, however, does not give attention to details of setting but rather focuses on the dramatic intensity, aiming to stir up the emotions of its listeners.

When Keats wrote "La Belle Dame Sans Merci," he was being influenced by the gothic literary tradition, most notably by the novelist, Matthew Lewis, author of *The Monk*. In his introduction to his book, Monk stated that "this grotesque school helped usher in the English Romantic Movement and debauched taste without ever really participating in the glories of the movement unless in the book before us."

Keats's ballad also was influenced by "medievalism"; in other words, it is very much a series of stories of unrequited love, an essential part of the courtly love tradition of the Middle Ages. Perhaps the most familiar medieval romance concerns the legendary King Arthur and the ideal society of fellowship among the knights of the Round Table. The knight was required to live by a code of bravery and honor known as chivalry. This code grew into an elaborate literary construction where the chivalrous knight was committed to a lifelong service of women. This art of courtly love required defending the woman's honor and, as seen in Keats's poem, a convention that mandated the lady would remain forever unattainable, despite the knight's unending devotion. Keats was strongly influenced by the fatal enchantress of Spenser's *Faerie Queene*, as well as by other traditional ballads concerning the destructiveness of love, such as those found in Percy's *Reliques of Ancient English Poetry* and Cary's translation of Dante's *Inferno* with its tale of doomed lovers.

"La Belle Dame Sans Merci" is a dramatic dialogue between the questioning voice and the knight in distress. It is also a poem based on two significant relationships in Keats's life, both of which had to do with an impossible love relationship.

In 1818, Keats's much beloved younger brother Tom died of tuberculosis. Keats, a devoted older brother, was in attendance all through the most difficult last months of Tom's illness. On April 15 of the following year, when Keats called on Tom's neighbors the Bentleys to collect the last of Tom's belongings, he discovered a strange collection of love letters. The tone of these letters ranged between lofty sentiment and outright vulgarity. They were from a mysterious woman named Amena, and they were purportedly written at the dictation of Tom's friend, Charles Wells. However, the next day, as Keats reflected on the content of these letters, it occurred to him that Amena never existed and that Tom was the victim of a great hoax. Indeed, the cruel joke went so far that Tom traveled to France to meet a woman who did not exist. Keats was outraged when he wrote to Wells: "I do not think death too bad for a villain. I will hang over his head like a sword by a hair." Many people of Keats's day believed that excessive emotion could be fatal, and Keats now became convinced that this evil trick had precipitated the consumption that caused Tom's tragic demise.

In the late fall of 1818, shortly before Tom's death, Keats also fell helplessly in love with Fanny Brawne, a pretty and vivacious girl of eighteen who had little interest in poetry, but who nonetheless genuinely returned his love. Keats's poem "The Eve of St. Agnes," a celebration of young love, can be read as a commentary on his relationship with Fanny. Though they became engaged sometime between October and December 1818, marriage was out of the question because of Keats's poverty, illness, and absolute dedication to his poetry. His love for Fanny became a source of anguish, and his letters to her attest to his anxieties and need to be assured. Ultimately, he knew his desire for Fanny would remain unfulfilled.

These autobiographical emotional tensions can be seen in "La Belle Dame Sans Merci." In the first three stanzas of the poem, the speaker questions the "knight at arms" who is described as "palely loitering." Thus, we immediately enter into a dramatic situation in which the knight is wandering aimlessly. Gone also are all signs of a peaceful and serene natural world. "The sedge has wither'd from the lake, / And no birds sing." In fact, there seems to be nothing left for the "woe-begone" knight to do: "The squirrel's granary is full, / And the harvest's done." In the knight's reply, which comprises the remaining nine brief stanzas of the poem, he recites a tale of enchantment by a lady, "[f]ull beautiful, a fairy's child," and tells of the honor he pays the lady and the efforts he goes to in his service to her. "I made a garland for her head, / And bracelets too, and fragrant Zone." (A "zone" was a belt or girdle.) Keats's knight, unlike the knights of medieval legend, does not perform any brave and daring feats but rather merely supplies the physical trappings of courtly love.

Indeed, the greatest physical danger takes place in the knight's dream. Having been lulled asleep by the "roots of relish sweet, / And honey wild," the knight has a dreadful vision in which an unidentified kingdom is held captive by an evil temptress. "I saw pale kings, and princes too, / Pale warriors, death pale were they all; They cried—'La belle dame sans merci / Hath thee in thrall!'" When he awakes, the knight finds himself on "the cold hill's side," and that, he explains, is why he is in the most abject state: "And this is why I sojourn here, / Alone and palely loitering."

Although there may be more than one reason for the speaker's troubled emotional state, "La Belle Dame Sans Merci" is a poem laden with anxiety. The key to this exists in the oft-repeated description of the knight forever "palely loitering." The poem ends with the knight emphasizing not his unrequited love but his need for reassurance from his feelings of apprehension and self-doubt. ❀

Critical Views on
"La Belle Dame Sans Merci"

MERVYN NICHOLSON ON THE FIGURE OF THE TRICKY
FEMALE IN THE POEM

[Mervyn Nicholson is the author of "Gertrude's Poison
Cup: Entering the Unknown World" (1997) and "The
Riddle of the Firecat" (1998). In the excerpt below from
another article, "Magic Food, Compulsive Eating, and
Power Poetics," Nicholson discusses the importance of food
as power in "La Belle Dame Sans Merci" and focuses on the
archetypal "Tricky Female" who destroys the knight's
masculine identity.]

> She found me roots of relish sweet,
> And honey wild, and manna dew,
> And sure in language strange she said
> "I love thee true."
>
> —John Keats
> "La Belle Dame sans Merci" (1820)

In John Keats's "La Belle Dame sans Merci" a beautiful woman with
faery powers destroys a knight. The knight is a vigorous male. He is
mounted on a "pacing steed," the horse being an image (1) of
masculinity, traditionally of (2) aristocracy, and therefore (3) of
power. The richness of imagery in "Belle Dame" is typical of Keats,
especially its appeal to senses other than the usual one of sight. For
example, taste, a comparatively undeveloped sense in literature, is
conspicuous. The beautiful lady finds at least three kinds of special
food for the knight's delectation: roots, honey, and manna. Indeed,
this is a poem about eating—and about *being* eaten. ⟨. . .⟩

In Keats the beautiful female feeds the knight with special food,
whereupon the knight becomes, effectively, food himself. In other
words, there is an exchange act: false food (in effect poison) for real
food. She trades food that is sweet—compulsively desirable—for the
knight's life-energy. The poem ends with the knight sucked dry, an
empty husk. Significantly, the knight, like the vatic poet in "Kubla
Khan," has a vision:

> I saw pale kings and princes too,
> Pale warriors, death-pale were they all;
> They cried, "La Belle Dame sans Merci
> Hath thee in thrall!"

The kings, princes, warriors are "pale," indeed "death-pale." Their blood is drained, as if the Lady were a vampire. Medically they present as anorexic:

> I saw their starved lips in the gloam,
> With horrid warning gaped wide,
> And I awoke, and found me here,
> On the cold hill's side.

Keats emphasizes this anorexic look: they are not only drained of blood but "starved." Their lips are shiveled. They are eaten—and cannot eat.

The Lady clearly collects males: masculine, powerful, vigorous men—kings, princes, warriors. She reduces these, the most powerful members of society, to bloodless shades in a Homeric-style Hades. Her literary ancestress is Circe: Odysseus's visit, during which he grapples with her metamorphic powers (and her magic food), coincides with his visit to the underworld. He feeds blood to the shades of Hades, a magic food that gives them speech. He then returns to Circe before pursuing his *nostos*, as if she contained the underworld within her. But whereas in Homer Odysseus does not merely disarm her, but wins a working relation with her, in Keats the knight and company eat, then are eaten, and then are suspended in a life-in-death state of lost power. He is now a shade, doomed to wander like Elpenor. Her cave, like the withered landscape itself, suggests a sinister womb (or even more sinister belly) to which the man now belongs—a dead nature enclosing a ghost.

In the usual course the knight would "feed" on the Lady's sexual vitality. For him to enjoy her would not warrant special notice. Yet this Knight, totally obsessed in a form of life-in-death, is now unable to self-transform, and so unable to live. Recall that life-in-death in Coleridge is a female figure—half gorgeous, half monstrous—one who metaphorically feeds on her victims, as Coleridge's imagery of fear sipping vampirically on the lifeblood of the Mariner implies. Now Keats's Knight is one who cannot eat—unlike the squirrel whose granary is full, or birds who have escaped the withered vegetation for the abundance of southern lands. The natural life cycle rolls on, regardless of the individual male's fate within it.

What Keats crystallizes in this poem is an old convention. A lovely lady, offering special food/drink, seduces a powerful man, then destroys him. The food is a crucial motif in this complex: it poisons, intoxicates, or causes unreal hallucinations or delusions of grandeur or pleasure. The food either symbolizes sexual pleasure or accompanies it. Compulsive food is typically sweet food. In literature, sweetness and sugar, like the related beauty, are associated with deception ("pie in the sky when you die"). They are also associated with transience: "sweet not lasting," as Laertes says, trying to make Ophelia forget Hamlet (Ophelia is linked to sweet food throughout *Hamlet*—"Sweets to the sweet"). Such food, being compulsive, is associated with obsessive states of mind, and to be obsessed is to be enslaved, to lose the power of choice. Compulsive eating is symbolized by intensely desired food objects.

The figure at the center of this symbolism may be called the Tricky Female, usually a witch. In the familiar Grimms tale of Hansel and Gretel, the wicked witch attracts lost children with her sugar-candy house. The children eat the house, but they are in fact in the initial phase of being digested themselves by a witch who cages the male to fatten him, to make him (not his female sibling) "dead meat." ⟨...⟩

The Tricky Female is deadly in a most complex manner. She does not merely destroy her victim physically. She also destroys his identity, the masculine force that constitutes his being. Keats's Dame crystallizes the figure of the Tricky Female, as well as, it seems, his own anxieties about female sexuality and about the food symbolism that permeates his work. But whatever his own anxieties (or however representative of men in general they may be), the Tricky Female is commonplace in literature, especially in romances, and in movies too. For example, in the film *The Maltese Falcon* an innocent-looking woman turns out to be a callous murderer who deceives men. The fearless hero, Sam Spade (played by Humphrey Bogart), unmasks her, revealing the murderous deathly nature concealed by her lovely body. She looks helpless, innocent, and, like so many maids in distress, intensely erotic, even seductive. Sarcastically calling her "Angel," he treats her at the end with firm brutality. As a Tricky Female, she is utterly unscrupulous and must be handled by someone deaf to her dangerous blandishments ("sweet talk"). This figure is a siren who lives by devouring males: a *Venus* fly-trap or black *widow*.

> —Mervyn Nicholson, "Magic Food, Compulsive Eating, and Power Poetics," in *Disorderly Eaters: Texts in Self-Empowerment*, Lilian R. Furst and Peter W. Graham, eds. (University Park, Pa.: The Pennsylvania State University Press, 1992): pp. 43, 45–47.

◎

JANE RABB COHEN ON KEATS'S REWORKING OF A LITERARY CONVENTION

[Jane Rabb Cohen is the author of "'A Melancholy Clown': The Relationship of Robert Seymour and Charles Dickens" (1971) and *Charles Dickens and His Original Illustrators* (1980). In the excerpt below from her article, "Keats's Humor in 'La Belle Dame Sans Merci,'" Cohen uses both Keats's journal entries and information concerning the spontaneous composition of the poem to support her thesis that the poem is a playful reworking of literary convention.]

The original journal letter context of "La belle dame sans merci" suggests an attempt by Keats to amuse himself and his intimate audience. The early publication history of the poem compounds its inherent ambiguity and obscures the impression that laughter, albeit close to tears, seems its initial catalyst. This heretical view may account for the composition's perplexing elements: the belle dame; the speaker; the knight and his dream; the revised versions; and its present reputation as an inexplicably haunting piece. No single view can define, but this singular one may illuminate "La belle dame," a poem which did not preoccupy Keats, though it raises many of his serious preoccupations. ⟨. . .⟩

"Wednesday Evening" abruptly introduces "La belle dame" rather than Keats's usual prose self-commentary. The spontaneous composition is replete with uninhibited misspellings, grammatical errors, and corrections. Keats again borrows the title of Chartier's poem, but the traditional heroine is scarcely recognizable. Her "merci," whose religious and erotic pretensions were undercut in "The Eve of St. Agnes," is more secular and modern, as its 1820 spelling in Hunt's *Indicator*, "mercy," suggests. There is no evil implicit in the possibility of the Lady's "faery" parentage nor in her appearance; if her eyes are "wild" so is the "honey" she brings her lover. Her "sweet moan" recalls Madeline's and her sorrow suggests regretful insight rather than malicious intent. The Lady sings "sidelong," but her indirection is unavoidable if she rides sidesaddle in proper romance fashion. Her gifts meet passion's demands, if not those of nutrition, yet in her "grot" she maternally lulls her lover to sleep. The wraiths may warn "La belle dame sans merci / Thee hath in thrall"; however, the Lady has done nothing sinister, and the words of phantoms interpreted by a dreamer cannot be accepted as wholly valid. "La belle dame" has not granted religious grace nor, perhaps, sexual consummation; but neither has anyone granted her pity, forgiveness, or gratitude. "La belle dame sans merci" resembles Keats's more loved and blessed "demon Poesy" rather than her archetypes in myth and folklore.

The "knight at a[r]ms" also defies convention, but he prompts laughter and pity if viewed as a self-caricature of his creator. Instead of engaging with hardy comrades in wordly "derring-do," this solitary warrior, exaggeratedly "haggard" and "woe begone," loiters. The hyperbolic "lilly" on his brow conspires with the "rose" on his cheeks to produce more amusement than sympathy. The "wasteland" setting suits his demeanor, but whether there are no birds or whether the birds present do not sing is unclear. Seasonal details round out the autumnal scene but unfeelingly imply that the knight's behavior is contrary to conventional process. ⟨. . .⟩

As observer and lover, the knight inspires little confidence. One cannot determine if the Lady he meets *is* or *is like* a "faery's child"; if her "wild" eyes suggest wickedness or sweetness, madness or inspiration, sorrow or joy; if she looked at the knight lovingly or "as" she did love; and if "in language strange" she indeed said "I love thee true." Her lover's blindness to all else and his growing passivity is amusing if not praiseworthy, as is his undiscriminating acceptance of her food and her tears. He shuts her eyes one minute and is himself lulled to sleep the next. But the humor of this juxtaposition is lost in the critical puzzlement over the significance about his intervening "kisses four." 〈. . .〉

—Jane Rabb Cohen, "Keats's Humor in 'La Belle Dame Sans Merci,'" *Keats-Shelley Journal* 17 (1968): pp. 10–12.

⊛

GRANT T. WEBSTER ON THE INFLUENCE OF THE *INFERNO*

[Grant T. Webster is the author of *The Republic of Letters: A History of Postwar American Literary Opinion* (1979). In the excerpt below from his article, "Keats's 'La Belle Dame': A New Source," Webster argues that Keats's use of Dante is indirect and, thus, requires a different interpretation than the traditional analogy to the fifth canto of the *Inferno*.]

Students of Keats's "La Belle Dame Sans Merci" have studied the genesis of the poem carefully, and one of their most commonly accepted sources is the fifth canto of Dante's *Inferno*. 〈. . .〉

But since there is only slight similarity between Canto V of the *Inferno* and "La Belle Dame"—Dante describes the region of hell where carnal sinners are kept, and tells the story of Paulo and Francesca, but there are no parallels of plot detail or phrase between the translation of Henry F. Cary that Keats owned and used and "La Belle Dame"—I should like to question this attribution and further note the similarity in the texts of Keats's poem and Thomas Sackville's famous "Induction" to the *Mirror for Magistrates*. I further propose that the link between Sackville and "La Belle Dame" is Thomas Warton's *History of English Poetry* (1774-81), where an eighteen-page commentary and summary of Dante is located in the middle of Warton's chapter on "Sackville's Induction to the Mirrour of Magistrates." 〈. . .〉 The implication of this line of reasoning is that Dante is connected to "La Belle Dame" only temporally, and is at best an analogue to it; and that the lengthy quotations from Sackville's "Induction" in Warton form a more important causal source for Keats's poem. The proof is found in the striking similarity between Wharton's text of Sackville and the text of Keats's poem.

Once the two poems are put side by side, a number of parallels force themselves upon the reader. There is, first, the winter setting of the action, which presents the stark situation of the narrator in natural imagery. Paralleling Keats's "The sedge has withered from the lake," the narrator in Sackville describes his own situation:

Eche thing, methought, with weping eye me tolde
The cruell season, bidding me withholde
Myselfe within: for I was gotten out
Into the feldes where as I walkt about.

More interesting, however, is the gloss the Sackville provides for Keats's line, "And then she wept and sighed full sore." This is the constant activity of the Lady of Sorrow, whom the narrator of the "Induction" encounters in the wintry fields. He describes her in these terms:

Her wealked face with wofull teares besprent,
Her colour pale, and, as it seemed her best,
In woe and playnt reposed was her rest:
And as the stone that droppes of water weares,
So dented were her cheekes with fall of teares.

There is a third parallel between Sackville and the *Indicator* version of "La Belle Dame"; the poem, first written in Keats's journal letter, was first published by Leigh Hunt in the *Indicator* of May 10, 1820, in a version which substitutes "wretched wight" for "knight at arms," and alters several lines in stanzas six, eight, and nine. This version has generally been regarded as aesthetically inferior to the original, and the fact that Keats approved the text has been explained, by W. J. Bate, as due to the fact that "the revisions were made when Keats was far too ill to have any confidence at all in his own judgment (early May, 1820)." I think Keats's approval of the change to "wretched wight," may stem in part at least, from his recollection during his own illness of "wight" in Sackville's Induction"; the Lady of Sorrow is called a "Piteous wight" and the word recurs throughout the poem.

⟨. . .⟩ The fifth parallel is the implicit gloss of the "Pale Kings, and Princes too / Pale warriors, death pale were they all"; Keats's fallen nobility are realistically presented in the fallen magistrates of the *Mirror*, who have been punished for the same kinds of earthly sin that beset Keats's knight at arms. ⟨. . .⟩ The two poems have in common, then, the same symbolic autumnal setting presented with many parallels of phrase; the same "wretched wight" as hero; the same sorrowful feminine figure; and the same final descent into hell.

If, on this evidence, we can accept Sackville's "Induction," as presented in Warton, as an important new source for Keats's "La Belle Dame Sans Merci," certain conclusions follow. First, Keats's poem is related more specifically to the descent into hell pattern of vision literature, and the "pale kings and princes" may be clearly identified as purgatorial figures. Second, the emendations in the *Indicator* version are not to be regarded as aberrant to the poem's meaning, even though we may dislike them artistically, and the knight at arms must be taken out of the courtly context of romance which the word "knight" implies, and should rather be read within the connotations of the "wretched wight" who is going through a purgatorial journey. Third, the extended gloss which the Lady of Sorrow provides for Keats's lady emphasizes the ominous aspect of her appearance instead of her role as temptress. And this emphasis implies further that the reason why the knight is lingering at the last, the "this" of "And this is why I sojourn here," is not because the lady as sexual temptress has left him alone, but because the lady as guide has left him in this hellish situation. In general, the placing of the poem in this descent into hell pattern of vision literature has the effect of emphasizing the mood of the frame stanzas—the wintry vision of Keats—and de-emphasizing the temptation stanzas.

—Grant T. Webster, "Keats's 'La Belle Dame': A New Source," *English Language Notes* 3, no. 1 (September 1965): pp. 42–46.

⟨☙⟩

JUDITH WEISSMAN ON THE NATURE OF LANGUAGE IN THE POEM

[Judith Weissman is the author of "Women without Meaning: Browning's Feminism" (1982) and "Dickens' Great Expectations: Pip's Arrested Development" (1981). In the excerpt below from her article, "'Language Strange': 'La Belle Dame Sans Merci' and the Language of Nature,"

Weissman maintains that in addition to its many enchanting features, the poem must also be read as an engagement with the Romantic debate on the nature of language.]

There is nothing in English Romantic poetry quite like Keats' "La Belle Dame Sans Merci"—so bare, so haunting, so close to the world of magic and fairy tales, so apparently free from the intellectual concerns of the poet. Even the simplest of the Lyrical Ballads, the ones most similar to "La Belle Dame Sans Merci" in form, contain some evidence of the poet's intellectual conversation with an implied adversary; they contain assertions—that children have wisdom which adults lose, or that passive joy is better than active thought. "La Belle Dame Sans Merci" is a more attractive poem than "We Are Seven" or "The Tables Turned" to readers who have been taught that didacticism is the mark of bad poetry; but I believe that in spite of its haunting beauty and apparent mystery, "La Belle Dame Sans Merci" is nevertheless also a part of a Romantic intellectual dialogue, a dialogue about whether nature has a language.

Sufficient critical attention has not been given to the key lines in the poem:

> And sure in language strange she said
> "I love thee true."

The knight is ensnared by the lady because he believes that he understands her language; but if the language is strange to him, he cannot know whether or not he actually understands it. "La Belle Dame Sans Merci" is Keats' defiance of his Romantic predecessors—Wordsworth, Coleridge, Byron, and Shelley—who all, at least at some point in their poetic careers, claimed to believe that they could understand the mysterious language of nature. Beneath the ballad is an argument, a statement that we only deceive ourselves by imagining that nature speaks a language which we can understand. ⟨...⟩

The mysterious language of Keats' fairy-woman is not a feature of the tales which are possible sources for his poem; and the many critics who have discussed the backgrounds of the poem have virtually ignored this striking fact, even though the obvious place to begin an interpretation of any new version of a traditional story is with the artist's additions or changes. The body of criticism on the poem is nevertheless immense and illuminating. Certainly our understanding of "La Belle Dame Sans Merci" is enriched by the work of scholars like Douglas Bush, Earl Wasserman, Harold Bloom, Mario D'Avanzo, and Stuart Sperry, who have discussed the relationship of Keats' poem to its many sources and analogues in both folk literature (Medieval ballads, Celtic fairy tales, Arthurian legend) and the work of writers like Dante, some of whose damned lovers resemble the knight, and Spenser, some of whose temptresses resemble the lady. And the poem can support most of the interpretations that have been offered. It can be read psychologically, in terms like those of Hyatt Williams, who sees the fairy-woman as a "Bad Breast Mother," or of Charles Patterson, who sees her as a Jungian anima figure. And it has, of course, also invited many Romantically traditional interpretations: To give a few examples, Mario D'Avanzo sees the woman as an emblem of the imagination itself; Stuart Sperry, of the bliss that cannot last on earth; Earl Wasserman, of the ideal which no mortal can absolutely attain; and Harold Bloom (whom I shall discuss in detail later), of the deceptive power of the natural world. Nevertheless, I believe that by neglecting the importance of the fairy-woman's language, critics have missed a clue that would clarify the meaning of the poem. Wasserman does notice that Keats adds the detail of the mysterious language, but does incorporate this fact into his interpretation; Walter Jackson Bate does say that "even as far as the reciprocation of his love is concerned it was he himself who interpreted her as responding, though in a language far from definite," but he leaves the poem as a vaguely elegiac ballad about the impossibility of communication between the human knight and the half-human fairy-woman.

The poem demands a clearer focus than it has been given. The fairy-woman offers a particular kind of transient bliss, a particular kind of imaginative experience—the joyful experience of communication with nature so desired by the English Romantic poets. ⟨. . .⟩ The poem begins with the anonymous speaker's vision of the suffering knight, wandering disconsolately in a late autumn landscape.

> O what can ail thee, Knight at arms,
>   Alone and palely loitering?
> The sedge has withered from the Lake
>   And no birds sing!
>
> O what can ail thee, Knight at arms,
>   So haggard, and so woebogone?

The squirrel's granary is full
And the harvest's done.

I see a lily on thy brow
With anguish moist and fever dew,
And on thy cheeks a fading rose
Fast withereth too.

The speaker, unlike the knight, sees the landscape in a double way; it is now barren, but it is also potentially rich, capable of supporting both natural and agricultural life. He assumes, both from the knight's manner of wandering and from his feverish complexion, that the knight feels lost and bewildered in the landscape and can neither accept nor leave it.

The rest of the poem is the knight's story of what ails him, his encounter with the mysterious temptress who led him through nature into her cave. ⟨. . .⟩ Although the knight says that the woman is a fairy's child—a figure apparently unique in English Romantic poetry—she is, despite her possible supernatural origin, remarkably similar to a very familiar figure in English Romantic poetry, the child-woman who serves as an intermediary between the poet and nature. Both the sketchy description of her—

Full beautiful—a faery's child,
Her hair was long, her foot was light,
And her eyes were wild—

⟨. . .⟩ Even though the words of the poem point to an origin for this figure in Wordsworth and Coleridge, whose guides are good, Bloom suggests that Keats' fairy-woman is analogous to a very different female guide into nature, Blake's Vala, who leads men into an inherently sterile natural world in which they are trapped. Although this suggestion is intriguing, it leaves us with two problems—the meaning of the echoes of Wordsworth and Coleridge and the uniqueness of this female figure in Keats' poetry. There is no other evidence that Keats shares Blake's belief in the collusion between the eternal Female and nature in the entrapment of men.

—Judith Weissman, "'Language Strange': 'La Belle Dame Sans Merci' and the Language of Nature," *Colby Library Quarterly* 16, no. 2 (June 1980): pp. 91–94.

[Theresa M. Kelley is the author of *Wordsworth's Revisionary Aesthetics* (1998) and "Wordsworth, Kant, and the Romantic Sublime" (1984). In the excerpt below from her article, "Poetics and the Politics of Reception: Keats's 'La Belle Dame Sans Merci,'" Kelley compares several versions of the poem and maintains that the more mature Keats is responding to those reviewers who criticized its artificiality.]

Keats's "La Belle Dame sans Merci" illustrates the lesson Keats chose to learn from reviewers who criticized the patently factitious rhyme and figuration of his first published poems. For his early critics, these features betray a Cockney poet's unjustified poetic ambition. For the mature Keats, they register the value of poetic craft and the status of the poet as maker. In "La Belle Dame sans Merci" Keats makes the strongest possible case for this view of his poetic task by presenting the belle dame as a figure whose otherness belongs to allegory, the most factitious of poetic figures. In doing so, he also acknowledges a line of poetic indebtedness and ambition that goes back to Spenser and allegorical romance.

In Keats's poem the knight and male chorus of kings, princes, and warriors claim that the belle dame has them in "thrall," even as her literary antecedents have enthralled their lovers. Although critics have rarely questioned this claim, it masks a prior entrapment. As the object of their dread and fascination, she is a fetish, a figure whose alien status is the product of a collective decision to name her "la belle dame sans merci." Her figurative capture suggests the reciprocal relation between capture and estrangement that exists in poetic figures whose otherness implies an allegorical rather than symbolic structure of meaning. By this I mean that as a figure she resists the instantaneous understanding Coleridge found in Romantic symbols, those figures whose tenor and vehicle are so closely bound (or so represented) that we understand their meaning immediately. As a poem whose central figure is defined by her antithetical relation to the speakers of the poem and to a long tradition of belle dames, Keats's "La Belle Dame sans Merci" explores the value of poetic figures whose meaning is not intuited but learned. As a figure the belle dramatizes what readers of traditional allegory assumed: an allegorical structure of meaning (whether or not the figure in question is part of a fully allegorical narrative) takes time to understand.

The allegorical otherness of Keats's belle dame indicates two ways we might understand the historical consciousness of Romantic figures. First, because the poem that bears her name is evidently riddled with signs of its indebtedness to earlier poems, it presents a strong, perhaps deliberately exaggerated, case for the poetic value of figures that acknowledge their history. Second, because her otherness is a provocative if half-evasive reply to Keats's early critics, the belle dame makes this reception history part of her meaning.

Read in these terms, Keats's belle dame suggests how poetic composition may be bound up with the exigencies of publication and critical reception as well as personal circumstance. Clearly the extent to which this mutual binding exists depends on the poet, the occasion for writing, and other circumstances of time, ideology, and place. Until recently, critics have argued that these considerations are marginal, if relevant at all, for reading Keats. Instead, they have often assumed that Keats achieved poetic greatness in part because he transcended the negative criticism that greeted his first published poems. A version of this assessment remains influential among post-structuralist critics. Thus Richard Macksey proposes that as Keats matured he abandoned "the chatty archaism" of his Cockney style to adopt a simpler, more serene style that renounced much, including the poetic indebtedness of earlier poems. ⟨. . .⟩

Of the two versions of "La Belle Dame sans Merci" that Keats composed, the early draft of April 1819 and the version published in *The Indicator* a little more than a year later, readers have usually preferred the former or, more precisely, one of three later transcripts made of it by Charles Brown and Richard Woodhouse. Claiming that Hunt unduly influenced Keats as he revised the poem for Hunt's periodical, most critics and editors have dismissed the *Indicator* version as aesthetically inferior. ⟨. . .⟩

In the *Indicator* version the "knight-at-arms" of the early draft became a "woeful wight," an archaic and generic term for a human being or, in this case, a man. Along with other revisions, this one makes the poem more emphatically a ballad about a doomed relationship between a faery woman and a mortal lover. In this version the belle dame shows more human fears—or at least more sadness—and the "wight's" response to her is more active, even slightly masterful as he "kisse[s her] to sleep." Unlike the knight, who is lulled to sleep by his faery lover, the wight reports that they both "slumbered on the moss."

Keats suggests the naturalized, human emphasis of the version by using the English spelling of "mercy" in the title and the text. Whereas the early draft and its later transcripts preserve the French spelling, in the *Indicator* text the belle dame is half-Englished, as she is in the translation of Alain Chartier's medieval poem of the same title, which Hunt's *Indicator* preface identifies, somewhat misleadingly, as Keats's source. Keats's substitution of "mercy" also replaces one ambiguity with another. The French *merci* may mean pity, compassion or thanks. In the chivalric context of Chartier's ballad, the "beautiful lady without pity" is she who refuses a lover— in effect, she shows no chivalric *politesse*, or says "no thanks." The English "mercy" of the *Indicator* text abandons the implied chivalric pun. Moreover, its presentation of a belle dame who seems less in control of the love relation encourages us to read her name and the title of the poem as a comment on her woeful predicament as well. Like the wight, she stands in need of the "mercy" neither can expect from a society threatened by her supernatural nature.

—Theresa M. Kelley, "Poetics and the Politics of Reception: Keats's 'La Belle Dame Sans Merci,'" *English Literary History* 54, no. 2 (Summer 1987): pp. 333–36.

Works by
John Keats

Poems by John Keats. 1817.

Endymion: A Poetical Romance. 1817.

The Fall of Hyperion. A Dream. 1819.

Lamia, Isabella, The Eve of St. Agnes and Other Poems. 1820.

The Letters of John Keats. Hyder Edward Rollins, ed. 1958.

The Poetical Works and Other Writings of John Keats. H. Buxton Forman, Maurice Buxton Forman, and John Masefield, eds. 1970.

The Letters of John Keats: A New Selection. Robert Gittings, ed. 1970.

The Complete Poems of John Keats. Miriam Allott, ed. 1995.

Works about
John Keats

Alwes, Karla. *Imagination Transformed: The Evolution of the Female Character in Keats's Poetry.* Carbondale: Southern Illinois University Press, 1993.

Aske, Martin. *Keats and Hellenism: An Essay.* New York: Cambridge University Press, 1985.

Barnard, John. *John Keats.* New York: Cambridge University Press, 1987.

Barth, Robert J., and John L. Mahoney, eds. *Coleridge, Keats and the Imagination: Romanticism and Adam's Dream: Essays in Honor of Walter Jackson Bate.* Columbia: University of Missouri Press, 1990.

Bate, Walter Jackson. *John Keats.* New York: Oxford University Press, 1966.

———. *Keats: A Collection of Critical Essays.* Englewood Cliffs, N.J.: Prentice-Hall, 1964.

Bennett, Andrew. *Keats, Narrative and Audience: The Posthumous Life of Writing.* New York: Cambridge University Press, 1994.

Bloom, Harold. *The Visionary Company: A Reading of English Romantic Poetry.* Ithaca: Cornell University Press, 1971.

Caldwell, James Ralston. *John Keats' Fancy: The Effect on Keats of the Psychology of his Day.* Ithaca, N.Y.: Cornell University Press, 1945.

De Almeida, Hermione. *Critical Essays on John Keats.* Boston: G. K. Hall, 1990.

Dickstein, Morris. *Keats and His Poetry: A Study in Development.* Chicago: University of Chicago Press, 1971.

Ende, Stuart A. *Keats and the Sublime.* New Haven: Yale University Press, 1976.

Evert, Walter H. *Aesthetic and Myth in the Poetry of Keats.* Princeton: Princeton University Press, 1965.

Gittings, Robert. *John Keats: The Living Year: 21 September, 1818 to 21 September, 1819.* Westport, Conn.: Greenwood Press, 1978.

Goellnicht, Donald C. *The Poet-Physician: Keats and Medical Science.* Pittsburgh: University of Pittsburgh Press, 1984.

Goldberg, Milton Allan. *The Poetics of Romanticism: Toward a Reading of John Keats.* Yellow Springs, Ohio: Antioch Press, 1969.

Goslee, Nancy Moore. *Uriel's Eye: Miltonic Stationing and Statuary in Blake, Keats and Shelley.* University, Ala.: University of Alabama Press, 1985.

Gradman, Barry. *Metamorphosis in Keats.* New York: New York University Press, 1980.

Hagstrum, Jean H. *The Romantic Body: Love and Sexuality in Keats, Wordsworth and Blake.* Knoxville: University of Tennessee Press, 1985.

Hilton, Timothy. *Keats and His World.* New York: Viking Press, 1971.

Hirst, Wolf Z. *John Keats.* Boston: Twayne, 1981.

Jack, Ian. *John Keats and the Mirror of Art.* Oxford: Clarendon Press, 1967.

Jones, James Land. *Adams' Dream: Mythic Consciousness in Keats and Yeats.* Athens: University of Georgia Press, 1975.

Jugurtha, Lillie. *Keats and Nature.* New York: Peter Lang, 1985.

Kucich, Greg. *Keats, Shelley and Romantic Spensarianism.* University Park: Pennsylvania State University Press, 1991.

Lau, Beth. *Keats's Reading of the Romantic Poets.* Ann Arbor: University of Michigan Press, 1991.

———. *Keats's Paradise Lost.* Gainesville: University Press of Florida, 1998.

Levinson, Marjorie. *Keats's Life of Allegory: The Origins of a Style.* New York: Blackwell, 1988.

Little, Judy. *Keats as a Narrative Poet: A Test of Invention.* Lincoln: University of Nebraska Press, 1975.

Lyons, Harvey T. *Keats' Well-Read Urn: An Introduction to Literary Method.* New York: Folcroft Press, 1970.

Matthey, François. *The Evolution of Keats's Structural Imagery.* Bern: Francke, 1974.

Minahan, John A. *Word Like a Bell: John Keats, Music and the Romantic Poet.* Kent, Ohio: Kent State University Press, 1992.

Mori, Masaki. *Epic Grandeur: Toward a Comparative Poetics of the Epic.* Albany: State University of New York Press, 1997.

Muir, Kenneth. *John Keats: A Reassessment*. Liverpool: Liverpool University Press, 1969.

O'Neill, Michael. *Keats: Bicentenary Readings*. Edinburgh: University of Edinburgh Press for the University of Durham, 1997.

O'Rourke, James L. *Keats's Odes and Contemporary Criticism*. Gainesville: University of Florida Press, 1998.

Perkins, David. *The Quest for Permanence: The Symbolism of Wordsworth, Shelley, and Keats*. Cambridge: Cambridge University Press, 1959.

Pollard, David. *The Poetry of Keats: Language and Experience*. Totowa, N.J.: Barnes & Noble, 1984.

Rees, Joan. *The Bright Star: The Story of John Keats and Fanny Brawne*. London: Harrap, 1968.

Ricks, Christopher B. *Keats and Embarrassment*. Oxford: Clarendon Press, 1974.

Robinson, Jeffrey Cane. *Reception and Poetics in Keats: My Ended Poet*. New York: St. Martin's Press, 1998.

Roe, Nicholas, ed. *Keats and History*. New York: Cambridge University Press, 1995.

———. *John Keats and the Culture of Dissent*. New York: Clarendon Press: Oxford University Press, 1997.

Ryan, Robert M. and Ronald A. Sharp. *The Persistence of Poetry: Bicentennial Essays on Keats*. Amherst: University of Massachusetts Press, 1998.

Rzepka, Charles J. *The Self as Mind: Vision and Identity in Wordsworth, Coleridge and Keats*. Cambridge, Mass.: Harvard University Press, 1986.

Sharp, Ronald A. *Keats, Skepticism and the Religion of Beauty*. Athens: University of Georgia Press, 1979.

Sider, Michael. *The Dialogic Keats: Time and History in the Major Poems*. Washington, D.C.: Catholic University of America, 1998.

Sperry, Stuart M. *Keats the Poet*. Princeton: Princeton University Press, 1994.

Stillinger, Jack. *Reading the Eve of St. Agnes: The Multiples of Complex Literary Transaction*. New York: Oxford University Press, 1999.

————. *The Hoodwinking of Madeline and Other Essays on Keats's Poems.* Urbana: University of Illinois Press, 1971.

Stone, Brian. *The Poetry of Keats.* New York: Penguin Books, 1992.

Van Ghent, Dorothy (Bendon). *Keats: The Myth of the Hero.* Princeton: Princeton University Press, 1983.

Vendler, Helen. *The Odes of John Keats.* Cambridge: Harvard University Press, 1983.

Waldoff, Leon. *Keats and the Silent Work of Imagination.* Urbana: University of Illinois Press, 1985.

Walker, Carol Kyros. *Walking North with Keats.* New Haven: Yale University Press, 1992.

Walsh, John Evangelist. *Darkling I Listen: The Last Days and Death of John Keats.* New York: St. Martin's Press, 1999.

Ward, Aileen. *John Keats: The Making of a Poet,* rev. ed. New York: Farrar, Straus and Giroux, 1986.

Wasserman, Earl Reeves. *The Finer Tone: Keats' Major Poems.* Baltimore: Johns Hopkins University Press, 1953.

White, Keith D. *John Keats and the Loss of Romantic Innocence.* Atlanta, Georgia: Rodopi, 1996.

White, R. S. *Keats as a Reader of Shakespeare.* Norman: University of Oklahoma Press, 1987.

Williams, Meg Harris. *Inspiration in Milton and Keats.* Totowa, N.J.: Barnes & Noble, 1982.

Wilson, Katharine Margaret. *The Nightingale and the Hawk: A Psychological Study of Keats' Ode.* New York: Barnes & Noble, 1965.

Zillman, Lawrence John. *John Keats and the Sonnet Tradition: A Critical and Comparative Study.* New York: Octagon Books, 1966.

Index of
Themes and Ideas